Diapers, Pacifiers, and Other Holy Things

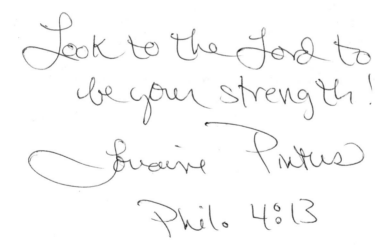

Look to the Lord to
be your strength!

Lorraine Pintus

Phil. 4:13

What do mothers have to say about this book?

"Reading this book is like sitting with a good friend who knows just what to say to encourage you." –Nebraska

"Thank you for helping me feel closer to God." –Mississippi

"I've got three children under age four. This book is saving my sanity." –Pennsylvania

"Ideal for personal devotions, Bible study and discussion groups, or for readings at baby showers." –California

"The short chapters are filled with good things to meditate on through my day." –Florida

"Friends wanted to borrow my book, but I can't bear to let it go, so I bought them their own copies. *Every* mother needs this book." –Virginia

Diapers, Pacifiers, and Other Holy Things

by Lorraine M. Pintus

Chariot Victor Publishing
A Division of Cook Communications

Chariot Victor Publishing,
a division of Cook Communications, Colorado Springs, Colorado 80918
Cook Communications, Paris, Ontario
Kingsway Communications, Eastbourne, England

DIAPERS, PACIFIERS, AND OTHER HOLY THINGS
© 1995 by Lorraine Pintus for text and Donna Kae Nelson for illustration

Cover Design: Cheryl Blum
Cover Illustration: Donna Kae Nelson
First printing 1995

        5 6 7 8 9 10 Printing/Year   03 02 01 00 99

Library of Congress Cataloging-in-Publication Data
Pintus, Lorraine.
        Diapers, pacifiers and other holy things / Lorraine Pintus
            p. cm.
        ISBN 0-7814-0246-8
        1. Mothers—Prayer books and devotions—English
    I. Title
    BV4847.P55   1996
    242'.6431—dc20   95-38741
                                                        CIP

*This book is dedicated to **Amanda** and **Megan**.*
I've already learned more from the two of you
than you'll ever learn from me,
*and to **Jackie Tiehen***
(Thanks, Mom. Pray my kids don't pay me back
for what I put you through.)

Acknowledgments

God has placed some extraordinary people in my life. Nothing tickles me more than to tell anyone who will listen just how much these friends mean to me.

Will the following people please come up one at a time and form a line so I can thank you? First I call on Jesus. I know, faithful Friend, that all things must begin with You. Next, Jan Walker. (How does it feel to stand next to Jesus, Jan?) Twenty years of your friendship is worth more to me than the world's supply of chocolate. Next, Tammy Ansari, my redheaded soul mate. Then Kit May. God has knit our hearts together like David and Jonathan. The four of you have loved me—and my children—with the kind of unconditional love that inspires greatness.

Next, some people with word wit: Lori Davis, Chelley Gring, Laura Davis, and my crazy, creative writing group: Scoti Springfield Domeij, Paul Moede, Becky Grosenbach, and Madalene Harris. (Madalene, what can I say? The highest compliment I can pay you is that there are no words.)

Now, those who have prayed. The women in the Thursday morning study at Woodman Valley Chapel and friends at Fellowship Bible Church and Tri-Lakes Chapel. You know who you are, so come on up. Then Judy Kahl, who is like a sister to me, and my own sisters, Melinda Hughes, Pam Connelly, Cindy Tiehen, and Julie Dunbar.

And finally, Peter, because in the end, you are always

there. No, don't get in line. Stand beside me. We belong together. I couldn't dedicate this book to you because it is a woman-thing, and you are all *man*. So instead, I dedicate to you my undying love.

Okay. Now that you are all here, I'm going to do something I've been wanting to do throughout the writing of this book.

Clap! Clap! Clap!

It may not seem like much, but in many countries, a standing ovation is the highest honor one can receive.

Contents

Contents (cont.)

How to
Use This Book

"*I* want a book with short chapters—something I can read while I breast-feed the baby," said Amy, mother of five.

Deanna, mother of three boys, agreed. "I read in the bathroom. It's the only time I'm alone. I've got ten minutes tops! If I can't get through a chapter in that amount of time, forget it. I don't need another thing in my life I can't finish!"

"I could use a dose of inspiration," sighed Sandy. "Lately, it seems like all I do is clean up messes and change stinky diapers. I need a book that reminds me that I *am* valuable, that what I am doing *is* important."

"What do I want in a book?" asked Mary, mother of twins. "I'd like a good laugh—and a good cry. I'd also like something that elevates my thinking above the level of a two year old's."

Anne, mother of a newborn, grinned. "I want to be made to think, too, but keep the message simple. My brain is numb from lack of sleep."

"I don't have time to read for leisure," added Pam, mother of three preschoolers. "Give me a book that talks about the things I deal with every day, ideas I can read in the morning and apply in the afternoon."

"I'm big on application, too," Kathy concurred, "but *please!* Don't hand me another 'how-to' book. They're so boring! Besides, I haven't seen a formula yet that works for every Mom. I want a book with real stories from a real Mom—her successes *and* failures."

Terri commented, "My relationship with God is very important to me. I'd like a book that will help me be a better Mom *and* a better Christian."

As I listened to the mothers in my MOPS (Mothers of Preschoolers) group, I thought, *These are things I want in a book, too!* I buckled my two preschoolers into their car seats and drove to the bookstore.

Three bookstores later I found everything I wanted . . . in *six* different books.

Buying all six books fell into the category of refinancing our home. The other alternative was to write a book myself, one that incorporated all the elements I—and other mothers—wanted. I blew the dust off my journalism degree, fired up my computer, and hammered out an outline for *Diapers, Pacifiers, and Other Holy Things.*

Writing a book is like having a baby. Initially it seems like a good idea, but in the final stages of labor, you moan, "What was I thinking?" Just when you think you can go no further, out pops a baby. As you gaze lovingly into the face of your child, you reach a startling conclusion. For all your grunting and groaning, for all the teeth-gritting, fist-clenching effort, *you* didn't give this child life. You merely delivered the life which God gave. You will care for the child, but he belongs to God.

A few birth facts: *Diapers, Pacifiers, and Other Holy Things* weighs in at thirty-one chapters. Each chapter tells a story. Most are true, personal experiences, but to keep from boring you ("Look! I found thirty-seven snapshots you've just *got* to see!"), I've tossed in several fiction and third-person pieces. Each chapter concludes with a Scripture reference and an application section called "Time Out."

Like the handy, dandy utility knife advertised on TV for $19.95, this versatile book has 101 uses. It's ideal for personal devotions, Bible studies for mothers with young children, readings at baby showers, conversation topics for play groups, teaching at MOPS meetings, or discussions for neighborhood coffees.

Study this book with other women. Or read it on your own. (I've found soaking in a bubble bath as a raspberry truffle melts in my mouth to be a highly effective reading technique.) However you choose to use this book, I pray it will tickle your funny bone, challenge your thinking, and inspire within you the need to walk more closely with God.

Section One: Baby Babble

"Anyone who lives on milk, being still an infant, is

not acquainted with the teaching about righteousness.

But solid food is for the mature, who by constant

use have trained themselves to distinguish good from

evil." —*Hebrews 5:13, 14*

Just a Moment, Please

"*I* am so frustrated I could scream," sobbed Terri, mother of two preschoolers. "Since having children, I feel like I've had to put my relationship with God on hold. Every time I sit down to pray or read the Bible, I get interrupted. How can I have quiet time with God when I have no *quiet time?*"

Terri had tried reading her Bible at night, but she dozed off after a full day of cooking, cleaning, and chasing after kids. Before giving in to her exhaustion, she set her alarm for 5:00 A.M. Early the next morning as she opened her Bible, three-year-old Jessica came into the room, rubbing sleepy eyes. Twenty minutes later Jessica once again rested quietly in her bed. Terri returned to her chair, picked up her Bible, and shot a prayer heavenward. *Please, Lord. Let that lullaby tape do the trick.* She turned to Galatians. Two verses later she heard, "Whaaa!" Greg was hungry. Quickly she nursed Greg and laid him back in his crib. Now it was 6:15 A.M. Maybe she could sneak in a few moments of prayer. She bowed her head and closed her eyes. A voice shouted, "Terri! Where's the breakfast cereal? Is it gone?"

Dutifully, Terri prepared breakfast for her husband. She fixed her sights on the kids' nap time. Maybe *then* she could have her devotions. No such luck. She spent most of Greg's nap time trying to get Jessica to be quiet. Just as Jessica settled down, the phone rang, waking up Greg. A friend wanted to know if Terri could watch her son for an hour while she went to an important doctor's appointment. Hearing the urgency in her friend's voice, how could Terri refuse?

No quiet time today. But there was always Sunday. Terri looked forward to the hour-long church service where the concerns of her world slipped away and she could focus on God. She glanced at her calendar and sighed. It was her turn for church nursery duty.

"Can't God see I'm *trying* to spend time with Him?" Terri cried. "The least He could do is cooperate by getting my kids to take naps at the same time!"

I hear you, Terri! The day Amanda was born was the day "quiet" took a leave of absence from my life. Six months later, I slumped on my bed amidst a pile of unfolded clothes and cried, *God, where are you? I miss You! It seems like ages since we've had a really good talk.*

Before having children, I reveled in hour-long quiet times with God. But caring for a new baby, learning to be a parent, and trying to be a good worker and a wife consumed all my time and energy. A yearning for the "carefree" moments I enjoyed less than a year before flooded my heart. Resolutely, I pushed the longing aside. Wading around in "what was" only added to my discontent. My life was different now. It was time I accepted it.

I love You, Lord, I prayed. *I want to spend time with You. But the days of hour-long quiet times with You are gone.*

God agreed. **You don't have an hour, Lorraine. But you have a moment!**

A moment? Yes, God. I have a moment. Nice talking to You. See you later. I've got a diaper to change and a toilet to scrub.

I pulled my weary body off the bed and opened the nursery door. I believed that spending time with God was more important than diaper changing and toilet scrubbing. But these chores had to be done. And if I didn't keep going, they wouldn't get done.

As I positioned the diaper under Amanda's tiny bottom, I heard the Lord say, **You have a moment.**

Yes, Lord, I do. Hi again! I sure spend a lot of time changing Amanda. Just like You've spent a lot of time changing me.

I chuckled over the analogy and headed for the toilet with my scrub brush.

You have a moment.

Yes, God, I do. Thanks for washing away my sins, just the way I'm washing away disgusting things in this toilet.

In the kitchen, I set the table for dinner.

You have a moment.

Yes, God. Thank You for food to eat and a roof over our heads.

I was beginning to get the idea. As I put the bread basket on the table, I thanked Jesus for being the bread of life. I set Amanda in her high chair and praised God for sitting on His throne in heaven. As water poured over the dirty dinner plates, I rejoiced that the blood of Christ was poured out for me.

The next day I wrote several Scriptures on note cards and taped them in strategic locations throughout the house; one by the changing table, several in the bathroom, one by the kitchen sink. Then I opened my Bible and placed it by the rocker so I could read a chapter while I nursed the baby. As I worked in the house, I listened to Christian radio.

Day after day, I worked hard to "take captive every thought to make it obedient to Christ" (II Cor. 10:5). Seeing God in every circumstance became easier, more natural. Then a strange thing happened. I began to sing! In the midst of mundane duties, God was allowing me to glimpse His glory. Even as I wiped spit up off the floor or cleaned strained peas off the wall, I rejoiced. I was in the presence of the living God.

Before having kids, I had compartmentalized God, sticking Him into time slots labeled *Bible Study, Quiet Time,* and *Church.* Now the compartment walls had fallen down. God spilled over into every moment of my life.

Ironic, isn't it? It took not having an hour with God to realize that I had the whole day with Him!

"We demolish arguments and every pretension that sets itself up against the knowledge of God, and we take captive every thought to make it obedient to Christ."
II Corinthians 10:5

Time Out

• Memorize II Corinthians 10:5. What does it mean to "take captive every thought to make it obedient to Christ"? How can you do this? What does the verse instruct you to do *before* you take your thoughts captive? What "arguments" and "pretensions" in your life raise themselves above the knowledge of God? How can you cast them down?

• Do you acknowledge God's presence in your everyday moments or do you confine Him to compartments labeled *Quiet Time* and *Church?* What does it mean to abide in Christ? (Read John 15.) How do you do this?

• In *The Practice of the Presence of God,* Brother Lawrence reveals that the most effective way he had for communicating with God was simply to do his ordinary work.[1] He believed it was a serious mistake to think of prayer time as being different from any other. When do you pray?

[1]Brother Lawrence, *The Practice of the Presence of God* (Grand Rapids, Mich.: Fleming H. Revell, 1967), p. 20.

Big Things,
Little Things

*F*or mothers, one of the most inspiring verses in the Bible is, "If you faithfully wipe your child's runny nose, I will give you a mansion."

Okay. I admit that's a pretty loose translation of Luke 19:17. The verse actually says, "Because you have been trustworthy in a very small matter, take charge of ten cities."

Still, the nose-wiping thing works for me. Either way, the message is the same: We must be faithful in little things if we expect to be responsible for big things.

Jesus continues, "Whoever can be trusted with very little can also be trusted with much, and whoever is dishonest with very little will also be dishonest with much" (Luke 16:10).

Last week at the grocery store, I was tempted to be dishonest in a little matter.

I am a thrifty shopper. (Please. Don't get behind me in the checkout line. I don't want to try your patience while the clerk totals my coupons!) I consider a shopping spree successful only if, after shopping specials and clipping coupons, I can go home with at least one item which cost me nothing.

So you can see why I was ecstatic over the spaghetti sauce.

The advertisement said, "Buy one jar, get one free." The store's policy would allow me to use two coupons;

both would be doubled. Total price for two jars of sauce: 26 cents. I was happier than a kitten with a string until I whipped out my coupons and noticed the fine print. "Good on 48-ounce *only*." Oh, no. The special was for the 30-ounce jars. Surely the manufacturer didn't *really* mean to exclude other sizes. Besides, what difference would a few ounces make?

"Whoever is dishonest with very little will also be dishonest with much." Rats. I wish I'd never memorized that verse. Then I could have handed over my coupons with a semi-clear conscience. It's not as if I were trying to use the coupon for a brand I didn't buy! I could give the coupons to the clerk anyway. He would never check the size. He would never know. Even if he did, he wouldn't care.

But God would know. God would care.

"Coupons?" asked the clerk.

"No," I sighed, and returned the unused slips of paper to my purse.

Little things matter to God. And I don't know anyone entrusted with more little things than a mother. You know the things I mean. That little everyday stuff that can drive you crazy.

Wash the clothes, dress the kids, mop the floor.
Make the beds, feed the pets, go to the store.
Read a story, write a letter, kiss a sore.
When you're done, do it again.
And do it again once more.
Look around, so much to do.
The house looks like an unkept zoo.
You sigh a bit,'cause you'll never be through
With "little things" that cry out to you.[1]

Do you ever throw your hands in the air and cry, "I'm not doing this anymore! Nothing ever *stays* done. What's the point?"

There is a point. Actually, two. The first point we've already discussed: God entrusts you with little things to teach you faithfulness in big things. The second point is this: *God wants you to see that each little thing you do can have eternal impact.*

In Matthew 25, Jesus offers some people a kingdom in heaven because they did little things. "Come, you who are blessed by my Father; take your inheritance, the kingdom prepared for you since the creation of the world. For I was hungry and you gave me something to eat, I was thirsty and you gave me something to drink, I was a stranger and you invited me in, I needed clothes and you clothed me" (Matt. 25:34-36).

The heaven-bound bunch were tongue-tied. They couldn't remember doing these things for Jesus.

Jesus said, "Whatever you did for one of the least of these brothers of mine, you did for me" (Matt. 25:40).

Reading that verse caused my toilet scrubbing, nose-wiping duties to take on a high and holy purpose.

Jesus, I prayed. *Do I understand You correctly? Are You saying that when I wash Amanda's hair or sew a button on my husband's jacket, it counts as doing it for You?*

Yes, He replied. **When you do these things in My name for those who love Me, you do it for Me.**

What if I serve turkey to the homeless at Thanksgiving?

Why are you doing it?

Honestly? Because my friends do it. If I'm not there, I'm afraid I'd seem uncaring.

It doesn't count.

Why not?

You desire praise from people rather than from God. You do this for your glory, not for Mine.

How about the lasagna for Kathy? Does that count?

Why did you make it?

She was sick and couldn't cook for her family. I appreciated the meal Tammy brought us when I had the flu. I wanted to return the favor. Besides, aren't You always telling us to care for one another?

It counts.

Really? You mean lasagna has some spiritual connection?

Not the lasagna. The motive. I tell you the truth, anyone who gives a cup of water in My name certainly won't lose his or her reward.

Reward? You mean there's a reward for doing these things? That's nice, Jesus. But I don't need a reward. I do these things because I love You.

Ahh! You are beginning to understand the importance of motive. Now, why do I speak to you about the importance of little things?

I think it is because You want me to see that every thing I do, no matter how small, can have eternal impact. *A word of encouragement to the postal clerk is encouragement to You. A wave to a stranger is a wave to You. A cup of water for Amanda is a drink for You, that is, if my motive is right.*

You have spoken well. Now, go. Follow My example. Do what I showed you to do.

What did Jesus do? The same things you and I do. He washed feet (John 13:5). He settled arguments (Mark 9:34, 35). He served a meal to others (John 6:11). In a way, He even cleaned house (John 2:15, 16).

Since the Creator of the universe humbled Himself to wash filthy feet, I can certainly wipe my daughter's dirty face. If Christ served bread to others, I can serve meatloaf to my family. If the Son of God willingly performed menial work rather than appointing someone else to do it, how can I complain about disinfecting the diaper pail?

Little things matter. If your motive is right, even nose-wiping can result in eternal rewards. And that, dear friends, is nothing to sneeze at!

"Whatever you do, work at it with all your heart,
as working for the Lord, not for men, since you know that
you will receive an inheritance from the Lord as a reward.
It is the Lord Christ you are serving."
Colossians 3:23,24

Time Out

• Motive is everything. Before doing anything, ask yourself, "Why am I doing this? For whom am I doing this? Would this please Jesus?"

• Have you ever told a friend "I'll pray for you" but failed to do it? Do you copy personal items on the photocopier at work? Do you exaggerate your charitable contributions on your income tax form? Name three "little things" in which you find yourself tempted to be dishonest. Ask God to keep you faithful.

• Look up *faithful* in the dictionary. What does it mean? Why does God want to build faithfulness in us? Whom do we emulate when we are faithful?

[1]When I wrote this ditty, the list of little things seemed long indeed.

Daddy's Lap

"Yyyeeeeaaaahhhh!"

The shriek shattered the silence.

I finished folding the last two towels in the laundry basket before making my way to Amanda's bedroom to investigate. No need for alarm. Amanda was not hurt. This was not a cry of pain, but a scream of frustration. She was at war with someone, or something, and she was losing the battle.

Peter was already in the room by the time I arrived. I peeked through the partially open door and watched my husband pull our distraught daughter into his arms. Amanda's foe lay wounded on the other side of the room, a tongue-tied sole with rubbery jaws bound by a frazzled lace. The mud mark on the wall was the only sign that the tennis shoe had put up a fight.

"Shoe-ing" herself was part of Amanda's fight for independence. Victory was afoot (pun intended). But in the end, the sneaker "de-feeted" her.

"Honey, when you need help, all you have to do is ask," Peter whispered as he gently stroked her hair. A sob, a sniff, a sigh, and Amanda snuggled deeper into his lap.

I studied daughter and dad, wrapped in each other's love.

Oh, the comfort of Daddy's lap! The strength of those big arms to hug away the cares of the world. The gentleness of a fatherly finger to wipe away tears. In Daddy's lap, life's battles vanished. Nothing existed but the warmth and nearness of the father.

Tears slid down my cheeks. The scene reminded me that I, too, needed to crawl into my Father's lap.

Being a child of God made God my Father—my "Abba" Papa. I often pictured Dad sitting in a big, comfortable chair, smiling and eagerly motioning for me to come and sit beside Him. But lately, urgent demands and the compelling need to check off my "to do" list won out. I'd race past Him and call over my shoulder, "Catch You later!" Disappointment filled His eyes, causing me to pause . . . but only long enough to shrug apologetically as I hurried on my way. Yes, Dad and I were long overdue for a heart-to-heart talk.

I grabbed my Bible and headed for the soft, blue chair in the quiet, out-of-the-way office. He was there, waiting. I crawled into His lap and cried.

Father, I've missed You. Forgive me for neglecting You. I didn't mean to. It's just that, well, like Amanda I've been busy fighting a battle—a losing battle of too little time and too much to do! I am so frustrated. No matter how hard I work, I can't keep up. My life is out of control!

Friends would have been surprised to hear me pray such a prayer. Often, others came to me for counsel because I appeared to have my life "together."

By God's grace, I juggled ten balls at once and did it pretty well simply because I had to. The skill of juggling was something I had learned from my own mother. When Dad died, Mom had become a single parent of four children, the youngest only a few months old. Mom's life was hard, but even under the most stressful conditions she kept going. "You do what you have to do," she told me on many occasions.

I adopted her motto. Regardless of what came my

way, I kept going. And going. And going. But lately, no matter how long I kept going, or how fast I moved, I couldn't keep up!

Projects piled up at work. Until I could hire additional staff, I had to do the work of three people. My babysitter quit. Finding child-care for Amanda turned out to be a second full-time job. The cat needed shots, the car needed gas, and mold was breeding in the refrigerator (this mold would serve as dinner unless I could get to the grocery store). And, hanging over my head was a pressing job I hated—ironing Pete's shirts.

The physical running around tired me, but even more exhausting was the emotional burden I carried for a friend going through counseling for being sexually abused as a child. She looked to me for support. "I wish I had your faith," she told me. "You are so strong."

Strong? At that moment, I felt anything but strong! A better word for me was *defeated.* I'd battled with life, and life had won.

Crying made me feel better. My Father cared. He listened. He comforted. But I needed more. I needed help. Peter's words to Amanda were true for me as well: "When you need help, all you have to do is ask."

Please, Father. Help? I don't have the strength to do all this myself.

His response was immediate. **The battle is not yours,** He said. **It is Mine.**

Ugh! The truth was like a punch in the stomach. (Have you ever had God's gentle words knock the wind right out of you?)

How many times had God warned me against taking on matters He had not called me to? Why did I feel as if anyone who needed help was somehow my responsibility? My take-charge personality was a blessing when God wanted to use me to get things done. But occasionally I'd adopt noble causes on my own and plunge forward without God. "I can handle this," I'd tell myself.

Wrong.

Self-effort is ultimately self-destruction. Self-effort short-circuits God's purposes, robs God of His rightful glory and leaves me exhausted. (Exhaustion is God's reminder that we are not resting in Him.)

I asked God to forgive me for trusting in my own strength rather than His.

"The battle is not yours, but God's. . . . You will not have to fight this battle. Take up your positions; stand firm and you will see the deliverance the LORD will give you" (II Chron. 20:15, 17).

God's words lifted my burden. Nothing changed. Everything changed. I closed my Bible and crawled down from my Father's lap, but during the day's skirmishes, I never let go of His hand.

Time Out

• What battles do you fight? List them on a piece of paper. Are you relying on your own strength or God's strength? Are you fighting a battle the Lord has not asked you to fight? If so, evacuate!

• Read II Chronicles 20. The Israelites defeated an army by standing still and trusting God. What is required to stand? What relationship do you see between standing and the psalmist's command in Psalm 46:10 to "be still, and know that I am God"?

• Memorize Deuteronomy 31:8. Be encouraged that in your battle, God goes before you and is with you.

The Cross
and the Pacifier

The Irish adore dummies. Germans love lutchers. The British ballyhoo their binkies. Americans prefer pacifiers.

In any language, a nipple on a ring means the same thing: salvation to weary, brain-dead parents desperately seeking peace.

Both my little suckers (no offense, Amanda and Megan) were pacifier addicts. Amanda insisted on 24-hour binky access. I bought one of those nifty clips that allowed the pacifier to dangle from her shirt like an abstract piece of jewelry. One day she unclipped the clip and binky escaped. Nothing, not even ice cream, calmed her cries until binky was once again tucked safely between her lips.

Megan was an obsessive, double-fisted plug pusher. At nap time, she clutched two pacifiers, one in each hand, which she alternately shoved in and out of her mouth. But aside from naps, Megan rarely used her pacifier. She crawled cheerfully through life, until . . .

"Help! Megan fell down the stairs!" Amanda shrieked.

I raced down the steps, gathered Megan in my arms and covered her with kisses. Sobbing, she pleaded, "I-I-I waaaant bin-in-ky." A moment later, binky bobbing in place, she was at peace.

Webster's Dictionary defines *pacifier* two ways: 1) a nipple or teething ring for babies; or 2) a person or thing that secures peace.

Peace. The perfect word to describe my girls with their

pacifiers. The perfect word to describe me with mine.

You didn't know I had a pacifier? I do!

My pacifier is not rubber, it is wooden. It's not a thing for sucking, but a thing for saving. It's not something I hang onto, but something God hung upon. My pacifier is (ready for this?) the cross of Christ.

Like Amanda, I have a constant need for my pacifier. Like Megan, the need for my pacifier is greatest when I fall. But I do not fall down stairs. I fall from heavenly fellowship. I do not suffer from surface bumps and bruises. I suffer from a pain deep within me—the pain of sin.

As a child, I thought sin was a bunch of things you "didn't do." Don't call people names. Don't pick on little kids. Don't steal cookies from the cookie jar. I remember being warned never to commit a "cardinal sin." I really thought this had something to do with red birds.

As a kid with little regard for spiritual things, sin was no big deal. As an adult seeking fellowship with a holy God, sin is a *really big deal.* . . .

Easter lilies adorned the pulpit. The church overflowed with worshipers who had come to celebrate the resurrection of Christ. As I sat next to my husband, I was a vision of loveliness (according to his compliment). New white suit with pearl buttons. Matching shoes. Nylons with no runs. (How perfect can you get?) And, it was a *great* hair day. I smiled. I sang. I prayed. On the outside, I looked great, but inside, I was a mess.

Black, ugly thoughts were snaking slowly in the direction of my heart.

I am sick and tired of being taken for granted, they hissed. The congregation sang, "Have Thine own way, Lord. Have Thine own way. Thou art the potter, I am the clay."[1]

I need a vacation. Let someone else do all the work. Maybe then I'll be appreciated. "Mold me and make me after Thy will, while I am waiting, yielded and still."

I think I will run away. Get in the car, drive, and never come back. "Have Thine own way, Lord. Have Thine own way. Wounded and weary, help me I pray."

It would serve them right. I don't need them. I don't need anyone. "Power all power, surely is Thine. Touch me and heal me, Savior divine."

I wish I were dead.

Gasp! Where had such an evil thought come from? How had I gone from having an innocent pity party to wishing I were dead? In answer, Sin sneered, "Gotcha."

I'd blown it. I should have put an end to those thoughts the instant they slithered into my mind. But I hadn't. Instead, I'd let them grow into a giant, fiery serpent coiled around my heart, squeezing, squeezing . . .

Above the singing congregation, I silently screamed, *Help!*

Immediately my Heavenly Father rushed to my side, gathered me in His arms and covered me with the kisses of His grace. Then He quieted my cries by giving me a pacifier, the cross of Christ.

On the cross, Jesus clenched my serpent in his fist. Slowly, the evil creature curled around Jesus' wrist, straining to stop the flow of blood in Jesus' arm. Still, Jesus refused to let go. "If You won't release me," hissed the viper, "then I will crush the life from Your lungs." Slowly his tail slithered across Jesus' back, over His ribs, around His side. Then, just as the muscles of the serpent tensed, Jesus tightened His grip around the serpent's neck. One final squeeze and the serpent dropped to the ground, dead.

On the cross, Jesus secured my peace, strangled my wretchedness, extinguished the fire in my soul.

The cross and the pacifier. When you think about it, they are not such different things.

> *"For God was pleased to have all his fullness dwell*
> *in him [Jesus], and through him to reconcile to himself*
> *all things, whether things on earth or things in heaven,*
> *by making peace through his blood, shed on the cross.*
> *Once you were alienated from God and were enemies in*
> *your minds because of your evil behavior. But now he*
> *has reconciled you by Christ's physical body through*
> *death to present you holy in his sight, without blemish*
> *and free from accusation."*
> *Colossians 1:20, 22 (emphasis mine)*

Time Out

• What happened at the cross? Read Romans 6 and 7. The Jews thought they had put Jesus to death, but Paul tells us it was actually sin that was put to death. Since sin is dead and Jesus is alive, what effect should this have on your life?

• "In the same way, count yourselves dead to sin but alive to God in Christ Jesus" (Rom. 6:11). Think of a sin with which you struggle. Repeat this verse but insert the thing you struggle with in place of the word *sin*. How does this change the way you view your sin? How can you experience being alive to God in Christ Jesus?

• Do you sometimes feel the tension of looking great on the outside but feeling "filthy" on the inside? How does

Jesus describe this inconsistency in Matthew 23:27, 28? According to I John 1:9, what should we do when evil thoughts take hold of us?

• The next time you see a child peacefully sucking on a pacifier, stop and thank God that He sent Jesus to pacify your sins by dying for you on a cross.

[1]Adelaide A. Pollard, "Have Thine Own Way," (Grand Rapids, Mich.: Hope Publishing Co., 1907, 1935).

Bubbles

*A*manda squished the strawberry in her hand. Red juice and pulp oozed over her knuckles and dripped down her wrist.

I wiped her up and gave her a juice bar. Tiny fingers slid across the smooth, icy surface. *Brrrrr!* She threw it on the floor, where it joined the rest of her lunch.

At eight months, Amanda was a student of touch, exploring her world through tiny fingers and busy hands. *Ouch!* A bristly brush. *Ahh!* Kitty's soft fur. *Ohh!* Mushy oatmeal.

After lunch I put Amanda down for a nap. I watched as she studied the pig floating above her head. Her hand stretched up, up, up. . . . Yes! She snatched the pig, setting it free, while the other barnyard animals jerked spastically on the rotating mobile. Triumphant giggles filled the nursery as she pondered her plastic prize.

For Amanda, life was a Disneyland of stimulating sensations. This evening she would experience the equivalent of a joy ride on Splash Mountain: her first bubble bath.

"Oooh," she cooed, as I sat her in a sea of fragile floating balls. Carefully, she scooped up a bubble and gazed in wonder through its watery walls. How beautiful!

Possessively, she hugged the bubble to her chest. Then, deciding to share her treasure with me, she lifted her hand to my face and unfolded her fingers.

Gasp! It was gone!

"Where's your bubble, Amanda?" I laughed.

Whimpering, she reached for another bubble. Pop!

"Whaaaaa!"

"Honey, it's okay," I consoled. "See? There are lots more bubbles."

I cupped a large bubble in my hand and presented it to her. She pushed my hand away and burst into tears. Angrily, she slapped the surface of the water, obliterating thousands of bubbles into a white film.

I watched, confused.

Why you are upset, wee one? Are you mad because the bubbles broke? Are you angry at the bubbles for disappearing? I wish you could talk so you could tell me what is wrong.

I studied her quivering lips and clenched fists. Suddenly, I understood. This was the first thing Amanda had grabbed that she could not hold on to. Plastic pigs, juice bars and strawberries were things she could clutch and touch. Not so with bubbles! Poor Amanda thought she had found something precious, but when she opened her hand, nothing was there.

I know how you feel, Amanda. I remember someone I once loved, and who I thought loved me, but one day he disappeared. For months I held on to the empty hope he would return. He never did.

I remember a dream. Corporate success. How I labored to climb that ladder! But when I got to the top, nothing was there.

I remember ambitions. Popularity. Power. Position. From a distance they were glimmering, magical cities, but each time I approached the gate, the city "popped."

Amanda, someday, when you are older, I will tell you a story of a little girl much like you. The girl was presented with two gifts, a bubble and a rock, one of which contained a hidden treasure. She could take only one gift as her own. Which would she choose? At first the girl was drawn to the bubble, certain that something so pretty would be perfect for keeping treasures. She raised her hand toward the shiny ball, but it floated beyond her grasp. This gave her time to think. If she wanted the bubble, she had to be willing to chase it. She looked at the rock. It was dull and unattractive. Still, it was within her reach, something she could hold on to. She chose the rock. As she examined it, sunlight reflected off its porous surface, revealing tiny pools of gold. She had chosen well.

Child, during these next few years I won't discourage you from chasing bubbles. It is fun and, I think, a natural activity for youth. But there will come a time when you must decide. Will you continue to chase bubbles? Or will you reach for the rock where your treasure is concealed?

Your rock has a name: Jesus. "See, I lay a stone in Zion, a chosen and precious cornerstone, and the one who trusts in him will never be put to shame. Now to you who believe, this stone is precious" (I Peter 2:6, 7).

My Rock is eternal. Bubbles are temporary. My Rock is solid. Bubbles have no substance. My Rock is worth more than a million costly jewels. Bubbles are a dime a dozen. Given all this, I wonder why choosing causes us any anxiety at all.

"For who is God besides the Lord?
And who is the Rock except our God?"
II Samuel 22:32

Time Out

• Make a list of everything you did today. In the sweat and effort of your day, was most of your activity bubble-based or rock-based? Read I Corinthians 3:10-15. Paul tells us that our work can be "wood, hay or straw" or "gold, silver and costly stones." What is he talking about? How can placing your work in these categories help you establish priorities?

• Read Matthew 7:24-27. How can you protect your home and family from experiencing the disaster described in these verses? What are you doing to build your life on solid ground?

• Read Psalm 18:1, 2; I Corinthians 10:4; I Peter 2:4-9. Why does the Bible describe the Lord as your Rock? Jesus is described as: 1) the living stone; 2) the cornerstone; 3) the rejected stone; and 4) the stumbling stone. What do each of these mean? Which of these terms means the most to you? Why?

An Open Door

*M*egan's curiosity opens doors. Bathroom vanity doors. Kitchen cupboard doors. Doors on my nightstand. She is certain that behind every door lies a magical playground created just for her.

But a dreadful ritual called "child-proofing" put an end to her fun. Now poor Megan's treasures are sealed behind closed doors. Anxiously, she waits, watching for an open door.

I reached for the scouring pad under the kitchen sink. Immediately, the "squish squish" of plastic diapers toddled toward me at an alarming rate.

Megan shoved my knees aside and squealed with delight.

Toy Heaven! Mouse traps. A putty knife. A bottle with pretty blue liquid in it. And, what was this? Mom's toilet cleaning glove!

Before I could intervene, she plunged all five rubber fingers into her mouth and began to chew.

"No, Megan," I admonished, tugging yellow appendages from clenched baby teeth. "Everything behind this door is off limits to you." I steered her toward the Tupperware cupboard, hoping she'd play with the toys behind Door Number Two. She wouldn't.

"Whaaaa!" Stomping feet. Drippy tears. Saggy lower lip. Her eyes accused: *"Mom, how can you be so mean?"* I tried to hug her, but she pushed me away.

Dear one, I'm sorry to spoil your fun, but you are going to have to learn: Children who rush through open doors without permission can get hurt.

The same is true for adults.

Adults often view favorable opportunities as "open doors." They charge ahead, thinking, "God opened this door for me. He must want me to go through it." Only later, after they've gotten into trouble, do they realize that they failed to seek God's permission before acting.

John and Melinda knew the house was extravagant, the monthly mortgage beyond their means, but this was their dream home! Impulsively, they put a contract on the house, reasoning that if God didn't want them to have it, He'd "close the door" by having the owner refuse their offer. The contract was accepted. Now Melinda works full-time. Their two young children spend nine hours a day in daycare. Pressure to pay bills has strained their marriage. Their dream home has become a burden. "Why is God putting us through this?" they moan.

Stan bolted through an open door. He didn't hesitate when his boss offered him a promotion because it meant more money. He quickly discovered it also meant more stress and overtime. He rarely sees his wife and children. Last week at a soccer game, Stan's son searched the bleachers for his father's face. Like the week before, Stan was not there.

Joshua plunged through an open door. As leader of the Israelite army after Moses died, Joshua was commanded by God to seize the land and destroy *all* the inhabitants. "Be careful not to make a treaty with those who live in the land where you are going, or they will be a snare among you," God warned in Exodus 34:12. As the conquering Israelite army marched forward, the people who lived there grew nervous. Fearful of extinction, the Gibeonites disguised themselves as foreigners and pleaded with Joshua to sign a treaty. Joshua "did not inquire of the LORD" (Josh. 9:14). He signed the treaty because, at that moment, it seemed a good idea. In his haste, Joshua disobeyed God and created problems for an entire nation.

Like Megan, John, Melinda, Stan, and Joshua, I've unwisely rushed through open doors and found myself in trouble. I'm learning that *God* must be the One who directs my life, not my circumstances.

Several years ago, as I was reading the Lord's instruction to Abraham in Genesis 12:1, "Leave your country, your people and your father's household and go to the land I will show you," God whispered clearly to my heart: **"Leave California and move to Colorado Springs."** The urgency of His words surprised me, even though Peter and I had been praying for several years about the possibility of moving and starting a marriage ministry.

Leaving California would be difficult. We faced many obstacles (call them "closed doors" if you like). We had no savings. We would give up well-paying jobs for no guaranteed income. We would trade comfortable surroundings for unfamiliar ones. Saying good-bye to family and long-time friends would be painful. We did not know where we would live, or if we could sell our home in such a depressed housing market. And I was not up to packing boxes after giving birth to Megan a few weeks earlier. (Moving with a two-month-old baby. Were we crazy?)

The door marked *Colorado Springs* seemed closed, but God had given us a key to open it called *faith*. Uncertain of what lay ahead, but certain it was God's will for us to go, we loaded the truck and headed east.

I could write a book about all that happened as a result of our move. God blessed us beyond all we could have dared to ask or dream. Within a week we had rented a lovely home, found an exciting church family, and settled into our work in the ministry.

Meanwhile, back in California, doors slammed shut at an alarming rate. The economy plummeted. The church in which we worshiped split over moral failure of the leadership. A major earthquake rocked our community, ripping the concrete in the patio of our former home a few weeks after we had sold it. In our case, the confirmation seemed to come *after* we acted.

God always blesses obedience, but sometimes the blessings are hard to recognize. Other times, for reasons known only to God, we are prevented from witnessing the blessings during our lifetime.

Jim and Elisabeth Elliot obeyed God's call to leave their home and go to Ecuador to tell the Auca Indians about Jesus Christ.

After months of less-than-encouraging results, Jim and four other men boldly waited on the banks of the Curaray River in an attempt to communicate with the primitive tribe. Their message of love was met with violence. All five comrades were murdered, their bloody bodies thrown into the river.

Had God opened a door for these missionaries only to slam it in their faces? It would seem so. But God says, "My thoughts are not your thoughts, neither are your ways my ways" (Isa. 55:8).

Elisabeth refused to let Jim's vision die with him. Courageously, she shared God's forgiveness with the men who had murdered her husband. The doors of eternity swung open as most of the Aucas received Jesus as their Savior.

What "open" or "closed" doors are before you? Are you confused about what you should do? God is not confused. He has a plan for your life. Are you willing to trust

Him, to follow His leading even if it doesn't make sense to you?

Consider these verses:

"I know, O LORD, that a man's life is not his own; it is not for man to direct his steps" (Jer. 10:23).

"I will instruct you and teach you in the way you should go" (Psalm 32:8).

"Trust in the LORD with all your heart and lean not on your own understanding; in all your ways acknowledge him, and he will make your paths straight" (Prov. 3:5, 6).

God delights in directing you. He may lead you through the wise counsel of a friend. He may instruct you through His Word or through a "gentle whisper" in your heart (I Kings 19:12).

Who knows? He may even open a door for you. Just make sure you get His permission before you walk through!

"These are the words of him who is holy and true, who holds the key of David. What he opens no one can shut, and what he shuts no one can open. I know your deeds. See, I have placed before you an open door that no one can shut."
Revelation 3:7, 8

Time Out

• Circumstances (open and shut doors) are only one way God provides direction in our lives. What are some other ways God directs you? (See Proverbs 11:14; 20:24; Psalm 119:105; Numbers 12:6; John 16:12; Judges 6:36-40.)

• Read Deuteronomy 5:29; Joshua 1:8, 9; Isaiah 48:17, 18 and Jeremiah 29:11, 12. Based on these verses, what results can you expect when you submit to God's plan for your life? What is the connection between knowing God's Word and receiving direction from God?

• God directs us in three ways: "go," "no," and "wait." Read Psalm 130:5, 6. What does it mean to wait upon the Lord? Why do you think God often asks us to wait?

Picture Perfect

*C*an I show you three snapshots of Megan when she was eighteen months old? I can tell by the expression on your face you'd rather sort laundry. Please, indulge me. If you look closely, I think you'll see something that will surprise you.

Here's the first one. Megan is crouched on her knees, her cherub face tilted upwards. That blurry thing she's clutching is my leg. I looked down at Megan, she looked up at me and, *click!* I caught her in the middle of a glorious grin. Notice the laughing face, the twinkle in her eye. I bet you can almost hear a giggle.

Isn't this one cute? The red dress with the lace collar was Megan's favorite. Her older sister wore it before her, and before that it was her friend Susie's. The power of Clorox on yellow baby drool never ceases to amaze me. The collar is bright, but it pales in comparison to the brightness of Megan's smile. She glows from within, as if someone stuck a light bulb inside her and turned it on. To get this picture, I quietly snuck up behind her, called her name, and snapped the picture as she turned to look at me.

Last snapshot. I hope you aren't offended by naked babies. Megan had just finished her bath. I rubbed lotion on her tummy, and she lost it. She squealed, giggled, and squirmed under my loving tickles. This picture captures more than a clean, happy baby in a fluffy towel. It captures the afterglow of a timeless moment between mother and daughter.

Now, study all three pictures. Megan's expression is the same in each. What do you think she is feeling?

I believe she feels . . . adoration. (Surprised?)

Adoration. Devotion. Worship. Reverence. For whom? For me! I know that sounds vain, but there is something deeply holy about the way small children look at their parents. In their innocent eyes, we can do no wrong. When we walk in a room, they light up and speed crawl toward us. When we pick them up, they coo our praises. If we put them down, they cry over the loss of our nearness and touch.

Megan does not look at strangers the way she looks at me. She knows I am different. I am her mother, the one who gave her life. I care for her needs. I love her so much I would die for her.

Megan's adoring spirit toward me is the same spirit I want to have toward God. He is my Father, the One who gave me life. He cares for my needs. He loves me so much He died for me.

When I look at my Father, I want Him to see in me a picture of childlike worship. I want Him to wave around a photograph of me and boast, "Look at My child! See the grin on her face? the twinkle in her eye? She gets that adoring expression every time she looks at Me."

Sadly, God has fewer of these kinds of snapshots than I'd like. Instead, blurry pictures show a frenzied, out-of-focus parent. *Click.* Me pushing half-dressed kids out the door, because I am late for a meeting. *Click.* Me frantically searching the freezer for something that will thaw and cook in two minutes. *Click.* Me slipping into church halfway through the sermon because the cat threw up on my coat.

Where are the pictures of me sitting at the feet of Jesus with an expression of adoration on my face?

Children eagerly crowded around Jesus. He said, "Let the little children come to me, and do not hinder them, for the kingdom of God belongs to such as these" (Mark 10:14). Then Jesus called to the adults huddled in the distance. "I tell you the truth, anyone who will not receive the kingdom of God like a little child will never enter it" (Mark 10:15).

That's convicting! I want to change. I want to be a child again, but how can I, with a thousand adult-type responsibilities clinging to me? Still, if Jesus commands me to become like a child again, it must be possible.

Perhaps the answer is staring back at me in those three pictures of Megan—total faith and trust that shows itself in all her unabashed yearning. I see that in her. And I think Jesus saw these qualities in the children that gathered around Him. When Jesus said He was the Son of God, the children believed Him, even when their parents did not. Days before Jesus' arrest, it was the children who praised Him in the temple, shouting, "Hosanna to the Son of David" (Matt. 21:15). Not long after, hardhearted adults shouted, "Crucify Him."

The children were drawn to Jesus, and He welcomed them with open arms. Unafraid, they crawled in His lap, touched His face, stroked His beard. Their trust invited nearness. Their nearness enabled them to touch God and be blessed by Him. What a contrast to the adults! They stood apart from Jesus. Arms folded. Skeptical. Critical. Untouchable.

Dear Father, I choose to be near You. Cultivate in me childlike faith and childlike trust. Cause these qualities to grow in such a way that I may one day present to You a photo album overflow-ing with pictures of a child adoring her Father.

Time Out

• Tape one of your baby pictures to the mirror in your bathroom. Each time you see it, ask God to give you a spir-it of childlike worship toward Him.

• Jesus continually gave honor to children in a society where they were often ignored. In addition to faith and trust, what other childlike qualities do you believe God desires to see in us? Refer to Matthew 18:4; 21:16; Mark 9:37; 9:42; 10:13-16; Luke 10:21.

• Do you complicate life by overanalyzing situations? How can you be more childlike in your faith? How is faith described in Hebrews 11:1?

Peek-a-Boo

*H*ide-and-seek and peek-a-boo are popular games at our house.

I count: "One, two, three . . ." Amanda ducks behind a chair. Eighteen-month-old Megan stands in the middle of the living room. Her tiny hands cover her eyes.

"Why isn't Megan hiding?" yells Amanda from behind the chair.

"She is, honey," I say. "Megan can't see us. So she thinks we can't see her."

I pull away one of Megan's hands.

"Peek-a-boo! I see you!"

Megan screams with delight and runs down the hall.

Hiding games are fun for children. But for adults, they can be painful.

Donna is thirty-five. She plays hide-and-seek every day. "I hide behind a smile," she admits. "That way no one will discover that my marriage is falling apart, that I'm going to counseling to work through the hatred I feel toward a father who abused me, or that I spend most of my hours crying and popping pills so I can escape the pain."

Most of us hide something. What do you hide?

Do you hide big things? Things you know are wrong and you're scared to death someone might find out? Maybe it's the bottle of vodka stashed behind the bread maker. The bruise on your child's face you caused in a fit of rage. The abortion you kept a secret.

Or do you hide little things, things you know are wrong but you fool yourself into believing are not *that* wrong? It might be parking in an illegal parking spot because you'll "only be a moment." Your envy toward a friend with a nicer house, kinder husband, or prettier complexion. The anger you feel toward a boss who fired your husband unjustly.

You think no one is watching, but you are wrong. You stand in plain sight of God. He sees everything you do. He is aware of your every thought. Still, you cover your eyes like Megan and pretend no one sees. The only one you fool is yourself.

"For a man's ways are in full view of the LORD, and he examines all his paths" (Prov. 5:21).

"There is nothing concealed that will not be disclosed, or hidden that will not be made known" (Luke 12:2).

" 'Can anyone hide in secret places so that I cannot see him?' declares the LORD" (Jer. 23:24).

"Nothing in all creation is hidden from God's sight. Everything is uncovered and laid bare before the eyes of him to whom we must give account" (Heb. 4:13).

Hide-and-seek may be the world's oldest game. It began with Adam and Eve. They passed the game down to their children, who taught it to their children. God frowned on the game, but many people in Scripture persisted in playing it.

David committed adultery with Bathsheba, then had her husband murdered. He covered his sin, and, for a while, he got away with it. Then God made David's actions known to Nathan the prophet. Nathan confronted David. "This is what the LORD says: 'Out of your own household I am going to bring calamity upon you. Before your very eyes I will take your wives and give them to one who is close to you, and he will lie with your wives in broad daylight. You did it in secret, but I will do this thing in broad daylight before all Israel'" (II Sam. 12:11, 12).

Hagar, servant of Abram's wife Sarai, hid from her mistress because Sarai mistreated her. Hagar fled to a desert, certain no one would find her. But God found her.

"Hagar, servant of Sarai, where have you come from, and where are you going?" He asked in Genesis 16:7.

God commanded Hagar to return to her mistress. He would bless her and her unborn child, whom He revealed would be a son. Awed by His omniscience, Hagar called God *El Roi*, which means the One who sees (Gen. 16:13).

Fourteen years later, Hagar again found herself in a desert, this time cast out with her son, Ishmael. When their water ran out, Death licked its lips expectantly. Just as Hagar thought the end had come, *El Roi*, the God who sees, "opened her eyes and she saw a well of water" (Gen. 21:19).

It is one thing to have a God who sees. It is quite another to have a God who opens your eyes for the ultimate purpose of meeting your needs.

If you are playing hide-and-seek, you need to know something. The game is over—and you lost. God found you. He's seen everything you've done, heard all your thoughts. And do you know what? He is not angry with you. He loves you. In the safety of that love, He wants you to pour your heart out to Him. Admit everything.

"When I kept silent, my bones wasted away through my groaning all day long. For day and night your hand was heavy upon me; my strength was sapped as in the heat of summer. Then I acknowledged my sin to you and did not cover up my iniquity. I said, 'I will confess my transgressions to the LORD'—and you forgave the guilt of my sin" (Psalm 32:3-5).

Confess your sin. Receive God's forgiveness. Only

then will you see the hope that lies beyond your hiding and be able to smile when you answer the question: "Where have you come from, and where are you going?" (Gen. 16:8).

As for hiding games, they're a losing proposition. If you want to play a game you can win, learn checkers.

"Teach me what I cannot see; if I have done wrong, I will not do so again" (Job 34:32).

> "*He who conceals his sins does not prosper,*
> *but whoever confesses and renounces them finds mercy.*"
> *Proverbs 28:13*

Time Out

• Read Genesis 3. Why did Adam and Eve hide? What was the result of their hiding? Who was affected by their sin?

• Read Jonah. Why did Jonah hide? How did Jonah's decision to hide affect others? What happened once Jonah acknowledged his sin and came out of hiding?

• Where have you come from, and where are you going?

• Ask God to make you aware of the things you hide (Job 34:32; Psalm 139:23, 24). Confess and renounce these things so you can enjoy sweet, free-flowing fellowship with God.

Life-Giver

"I can't do this!" I screamed.

Peter watched with concern. We had dreamed of this moment as being, well . . . romantic. It was anything but that.

I stared at the hospital ceiling through bloodshot eyes. Patches of tangled, matted hair clung to my sweaty forehead. An enormous white belly loomed above my chest. (Was this me?) My breath smelled like a sewer.

Peter reached for my hand. I pushed it away. So much for romance. "This is all your fault," I fumed.

"Come on, Lorraine," urged a masked nurse. "Push."

Push? Say that one more time, Nurse Starched Jacket, and I'll push you . . . right out the door! You have some nerve telling me to push. You go two days without food or sleep. You endure thirty-eight hours of nonstop contractions ripping through your body. You suffer the humiliation of every stranger in the hospital peeking between your legs and saying, "Hmmm. Doesn't look so good." Push? I don't even have the strength to breathe. All I want to do is sleep. Slip into the blackness. Sleep, sleep . . . forever.

I cursed the labor, but it had been no worse than the pregnancy. Two weeks after conceiving, a gut-wrenched nausea seized me, confining me to bed for seven months. I threw up constantly. My weight plummeted. Twice I was rushed to the hospital—once for dehydration, once for kidney stones.

A contraction measuring 12.0 on the Richter scale

shook me, reminding me that my ordeal continued. But I was finished. Kaput. I had nothing left to give. It was a cruel joke. My body, bursting with life, was lifeless.

"I will greatly increase your pains in childbearing." No joke. Thanks a heap, Eve.

Worry creased Peter's brow. "Honey, you can do it. Don't give up now. Please?"

I looked into Peter's pleading eyes. That's when it happened. A wellspring of determination, a supernatural energy that could have come only from God, surged through me. With all that newfound power, I pushed, and Megan was born.

Doctors would have us believe that when the baby is delivered, the life-giving process is complete. Not so. At this point, life-giving begins.

As a woman, you are a life-giver. That is why God gave you breasts and a womb. But don't be fooled into thinking that life-giving is restricted to what Scarlett O'Hara's servant girl, Prissy, referred to as "bringin' babies." Giving life is something you do every day. By the words you speak, through the warmth of your home, in the tenderness of your hug, by the wisdom of your instruction, through the stew on your stove. In all you do, you give life, not only to your children, but to everyone around you. (Be encouraged, friend. Even if you are physically unable to bear children, you are a life-giver!)

Giving life is difficult. It requires labor—not for nine months, but for as long as your child lives. With each new stage of your child's growth, you feel a new stretch mark, experience a different kind of pain. Sometimes the pains are far apart. Other times they come one right after another. Certain pains you ignore. Others crumple you to the floor, and you moan, "I'll never live through this."

In the middle of those mammoth-sized contractions, I

find the words of my childbirth instructor helpful. "Relax. Take a deep breath. Fix your eyes on your focal point. (In the hospital my focal point was a shot of a tanned beauty floating across a pool of blue water. Now it is Jesus.) Don't tense up; it only makes the pain worse. Visualize that future moment when you can touch the life you are now bearing and your labor is a numb memory."

Without labor, there is no life. We accept the pain because it accomplishes the purpose.

There is another process we must also accept if we are to give life—the cutting of the umbilical cord.

Think back to the birth of your child. Remember that final push? Your child's first cry? Then your doctor said, "Nurse. Bring in those four-foot hedge clippers. I want to cut this umbilical cord with one snip."

He didn't say that? He didn't use the quick clip technique? (Probably not. Instrument sterilization would have been a nightmare.)

Normally, cutting the umbilical cord happens something like this. A razor-sharp blade is placed on the cord. Pressure is applied. One by one the blade cuts through the layers of tissue until the connection is severed.

Fortunately, there are no nerve endings in the umbilical cord, so the physical cutting of the cord doesn't hurt. But the cutting of the "emotional" umbilical cord can be quite painful. You leave your child with a baby-sitter for the first time. As you walk out the door, you feel a stab of pain as the knife cuts the first layer of the connecting cord. The day he takes his first step (away from you), the blade cuts deeper. He learns to ride a bike. Outwardly you cheer him on. Inwardly you feel the back-and-forth motion of the knife. Then a painful slash—the child who has clung to you like plastic wrap for five years pulls himself free and runs eagerly into the arms of his kindergarten teacher. With each event, each new act of independence, the knife cuts deeper. One day eighteen candles light the cake, and you realize the cord hangs by a thread.

Like a man with an amputated leg, you will still feel the presence of the cord even after it has been cut. Mothers who wave good-bye to their children on a college campus tell me it is nearly impossible to describe what they feel. There's an ache. A loss. But mingled with the sadness is a strange sense of peace at knowing this was what God intended all along. To give life, and give life, until the life you have given takes on a life of its own.

Any way you slice it, being a Mom is tough. It's a double-edged sword. One edge is the pain. The other edge is the indescribable joy that comes as you give life to your children.

"I can't do this!" I no longer scream these words in moments of intense pain; I whisper them every day. In fact, I start each morning by acknowledging to God that I can do nothing in my own strength, but "I can do everything through him who gives me strength" (Phil. 4:13).

What else can I do but pray, *Dear Father, keep me dependent upon You. Only in Your grace and Your strength will I be what You have called me to be—a life-giver.*

> " '*My grace is sufficient for you, for my power is*
> *made perfect in weakness.' . . . That is why, for*
> *Christ's sake, I delight in weaknesses, in insults,*
> *in hardships, in persecutions, in difficulties.*
> *For when I am weak, then I am strong.*"
> *II Corinthians 12:9, 10*

Time Out

• Do you see yourself as a life-giver? Make a list of the ways in which you give life. List some of the people who benefit from your life-giving.

• Are you feeling pain as a result of something your child is doing? Describe the pain and the reason for it. How can you apply the words of my childbirth instructor to help you get through this difficult time?

• In what ways are you cutting the cord with your child? Why is this necessary? How is your child affected if you refuse to cut the cord?

Precious Baby Girl

ONE HOUR

"Hello, you red, wet bundle of wiggles. I am your Mom. And you are my miracle."

TWO MONTHS

Sweet dreams. We are both satisfied. Even in my sleepless stupor, I cherish our 2 A.M. moments together.

SIX MONTHS

"Peek-a-boo! I found you!" (I followed your trail of drool.)

EIGHT MONTHS

Who is that behind those bright blue eyes? You? Careful. Your personality is escaping!

EIGHTEEN MONTHS

You are more active than a verb. Run. Explore. Grab. Open (you). Close (me). How did you figure out those child-proof locks, anyway?

TWO YEARS

"No, you may not have candy for breakfast. No, you can't play with Daddy's razor. No, you may not unbuckle your car seat while I'm driving."

THREE YEARS

Stop! This is happening too fast! No more growing. I'm pressing the "pause" button of your life.

Where is my baby? What happened to my bundle of sweetness wrapped in pink blankets? Wasn't it yesterday you sought the comfort of my breast? Wasn't it this morning I stroked your fuzzy head and you gurgled your first smile?

I watched you roll over. Maybe I shouldn't have cheered so loudly, because next thing I knew, you began to crawl. *Okay, this is nice,* I thought. But it wasn't enough for you. You had to go and walk.

Wait. Where do you think you are going? Why are you headed towards that door labeled *Toddler?* Don't open that door. I said, DON'T OPEN THAT DOOR! You can't go in there by yourself; it's not safe. Wait a minute. I'm coming. . . .

In the doorway, I pause and look over my shoulder. Rocking horse pictures and a cross-stitch quilt decorate the walls of the room marked *Baby.* I can't bring myself to close the door on baby-powder smells, lullaby melodies, and soft pajama sleepers. I can't bear to walk away from white eyelet blankets and stuffed teddy bears.

How did this happen? When did your coos become words and your legs become wings? Where are you, precious darling? Are you hiding inside that determined three year old running stubbornly in the other direction?

I don't like this. Always before, my arms were full of you. Now they are empty. Heavy. Limply hanging by my sides. But one day a little girl will seek comfort when she falls from her bike. One day a teenager will need consoling after suffering a broken heart. One day a young lady will need help with her own baby. When that time comes, my arms will be ready. Until then, I will embrace every moment of your youthfulness, hug each slice of life we share. When you need me, I will be there to hold you, but I will not hold onto you. It wouldn't be right.

Click!

I shut the door. I had to. You are no longer a baby.

You are a toddler. I accept your growth. I will go forward with you. I promise always to treat you with the respect your age deserves. But as your mother, I reserve the right to silently cradle your infancy in the deepest part of my heart, because, no matter how big you grow, you will always be my precious baby girl.

"And the child grew and became strong; he was filled with wisdom, and the grace of God was upon him."
Luke 2:40

Time Out

• Luke 2:19 says that Mary studied the events of Jesus' infancy and "treasured up all these things and pondered them in her heart." What fond memories do you have of your child when he or she was a baby? What are you doing to record these memories? (Suggestions: keep a journal or scrapbook, take pictures or videos, or jot those cute comments and episodes down on your calendar).

• Find a box and label it "Baby Items to Keep." Select several toys and pieces of clothing that hold special significance for you or your child. Store these mementos with the intention of presenting them to your son or daughter as a graduation, wedding, or new-baby-of-your-own gift. (To cut down on the natural acids that age clothing, wrap the clothes in a newly washed cotton sheet and replace it with a fresh sheet each year.)

• Tonight as your children sleep, go into their rooms, place your hand on their heads and say a blessing over them. Ask God to protect your children as they grow and to help you, as a mother, to be sensitive to their needs.

Section Two: Toddler Talk

"Grow in the grace and knowledge of our Lord and

Savior Jesus Christ." —*II Peter 3:18*

Attitude of Gratitude

I stomped up to Customer Service and slammed the trash bag on the counter.

"I want to exchange this," I demanded.

A meek girl with uneven pigtails peered into the sack.

"I'm not sure we carry this item," she apologized. "What exactly is it?"

"A Bad Attitude," I huffed. *Stupid clerk. Couldn't she read the writing on the box?*

"We stock several types of Bad Attitudes," she chirped. "But I don't think we carry this model."

"I got this Bad Attitude at your store last year. It can't possibly be outdated." I pointed to the "Exchange Policy" posted on the wall. "You promise complete satisfaction. I am not satisfied with this product, and you had better do something about it."

Then I saw the sticker on Pigtail's name tag: "Be Patient with Me. . . . I'm in Training." *Just my luck.*

"Are you a mother?" I challenged.

"No," she said. Then I realized she wasn't stupid; she just didn't understand.

"Pretend for a moment that your boss tells you that you have to meet the needs of every customer in the store day after day . . . with *no* pay. And whatever they want—a glass of water, a book, or a different outfit—*you* have to get it for them.

"Now, imagine you have a 'wet clean up' in aisle

seven, a baby screaming at register two, and a 'customer needs assistance in Toys'—all at the same time!"

Pigtails winced.

"And," I continued, "you have to go to the bathroom. So you frantically meet customer emergencies until you have an emergency yourself and race for the little stall. As you sit, hoping for a moment of peace, a head pokes under the door and shouts, 'Two kids are stuck in the revolving door and the boss needs you on the floor—*now!*'

"What do you do?" I demanded.

The bewildered clerk shook her head. By the frantic look on her face, I knew she was beginning to understand what mothers face every day.

"You get one of these," I snarled, pulling the Bad Attitude out of the trash bag.

She nodded empathetically.

"But this Bad Attitude doesn't work, so I want to exchange it for something that *does* work." I shoved the box into her hands.

Pigtails reached under the counter for a form and promptly recorded my name and address.

"Reason for exchange?" she inquired.

"Not satisfied," I snapped.

She wrote my answer on the form.

"Item to exchange for?" she asked.

"A Good Attitude," I sighed, hoping the exchange would make my life easier.

"Sign here." She gave me a copy of the receipt and informed me I could pick up my exchange at counter three.

A cheery grandma beamed at me from counter three as she eyed my receipt.

"Ohhh, darlin'. You are just going to luuuuv this," she crooned. She knelt down and retrieved a beautiful gold box with a fluffy silver bow.

I didn't have to look inside to know that it contained something priceless. My Bad Attitude was cheap. Surely I would have to pay a price for the difference.

"I have one just like this," she confided. "I don't see how anyone can live without a God Attitude."

God Attitude? I looked at the receipt. The clerk had left an *o* out of the word *Good*.

"There's been a mistake," I stammered, trying to point out the spelling error.

"Land sakes, child! There is no mistake. See? Your name is written all over this box! In fact, we've been holding it for over a year, just waiting for you to come by and pick it up."

"And," she grinned, "all God Attitudes come with a lifetime guarantee. Now rush home and try it out on your children."

I waved to her over my shoulder. The lift in my spirit and the bounce in my step affirmed what I already knew: This God Attitude would work.

"Do everything without complaining or arguing, so that you may become blameless and pure, children of God without fault in a crooked and depraved generation in which you shine like stars in the universe."
Philippians 2:14, 15

Time Out

• Read Jonah 1-4. Describe Jonah's bad attitude and the reason for it. Was his attitude justified? How did God respond to Jonah?

• What do you do when your children have bad attitudes? Can we expect God to discipline us when we have a bad attitude? Read Hebrews 12:5-11. Why (and how) does God discipline us?

• How can you exchange a bad attitude for a God attitude? Psalm 57 may give you some insight. Notice that David begins the psalm with a bad attitude (poor me!), but ends with a God attitude (wonderful Lord!).

Good Girl

"Mommy, Megan is eating your plant."

I poked my head into the living room. A mound of black dirt darkened the light carpet. Megan sat on top of the mound, chewing on a palm frond. Several branches lay scattered about the room.

She smiled at me, a sweet, dirty grin.

"Oh, Megan. Why did you do that?" I sighed. I unwound green things from her fingers and put her in her playpen where she could do no further damage.

Amanda climbed onto the stool by the sink and watched me repot what was left of the plant. Her brow wrinkled, deep in thought. *Oh no. She had "The Look."* Whenever she got "The Look," I got questions I couldn't answer. Yesterday it was, "When kitties die, do they go to heaven?" The time before that, "Can God play the guitar?" and "Does God want us to love Satan?"

I prayed for wisdom. I would need it.

"Mommy, do you still love Megan?" Amanda asked.

"Of course," I said. (Hey, this question wasn't so tough.) "What makes you think I don't love her?"

" 'Cause she was a bad girl for breaking your plant."

Hmmm. This was a bit tougher. Amanda sensed a connection between love and behavior. Good behavior equals love, she had decided. What does bad behavior equal?

As a child, I struggled with the same question. When I got good grades, cleaned my room, and showed kindness to others, friends, and relatives freely passed out "I love you's." But when I bit my brother, tore my new dress, or talked back to Mom, I faced a scolding silence. No words were spoken, but I heard "you don't deserve to be loved."

Love was something you earned, I concluded. No one ever told me this. I believed it true because my experience proved it true. Perform well, work hard, be good, and everyone loved you. Screw up and cry alone.

For twenty-three years I worked to earn people's love. Then God introduced me to a new kind of love. Unconditional love. Not the kind of love that says, "I love you if . . ." Or "I love you when . . ." But the kind of love that says, "I love you." Period.

I tested God's love for me. I did bad things, things I knew disappointed Him. Still He assured me, "I love you." I failed Him and turned my back on Him, but He continued to love me. This kind of love was difficult to receive. I felt so unworthy! It seemed when I deserved love the least, He loved me the most. Eventually, my resistance to His love broke, and I was set free. Free from my performance-oriented nature that left me forever wanting. Free to love and be loved in a deeper way than I had ever known before.

Unconditional love. I longed for Amanda to experience this early in her life, to be spared the pain I felt as a child. How could I help Amanda see that just because someone does something bad that doesn't make the person undeserving of love?

I looked deliberately into her eyes and chose my words carefully.

"Honey, Megan did a bad thing. But that doesn't make her a bad girl. She is a good girl."

"Separate who a person is from what that person does," Christian counselors tell us. "Reject sinful behavior;

love the individual," pastors say. Once people can do this, it is easier for them to accept being loved simply for who they are.

Tough concept. Did Amanda get it?

"But, Mommy, do you still love Megan?" she pressed.

Maybe if I tried another approach.

"Honey, even if Megan did the most terrible thing in the world, I would still love her," I said.

Unconvinced, Amanda contrived the worst crime she could imagine. "Would you still love Megan even if she ate cookies in her bed, and then wet in it?"

"Yes, Amanda. Even if she did that, I would still love her."

"Why?" (Amanda's favorite question.)

"Because I'm her mother." (My favorite response.)

For some reason, this satisfied her, and she skipped off to play.

Lesson over for Amanda, but not for me.

If I spent every waking moment exploring God's love for me, I'd still never know all its dimensions, never bump into a boundary. As Paul said, "I pray that you . . . may . . . grasp how wide and long and high and deep is the love of Christ" (Eph. 3:17, 18).

Why does God love me? Not for my accomplishments. Not because I read my Bible. Not because I give clothes to the poor or money to the church. He loves me because I am me. Nothing I can ever do will make God love me more—or less—than He already does. Now that I have children, I can see how this is possible. Nothing Amanda or Megan could ever do would keep me from loving them or make me love them more.

Two years have passed since my conversation with Amanda. She continues to amaze me in her understanding of my love for her, and God's love for her.

And Megan? Can a three year old understand unconditional love?

Yesterday as we were riding in the car I asked,
"Megan, do you think I love you?"

Her face lit up. Playfully she teased, "Silly Mommy. Of
course you love me."

"Why do you think so?"

She answered simply, "Because you just do."

Good answer. God's answer. To you.

"But God demonstrates his own love for us in this:
While we were still sinners, Christ died for us."
Romans 5:8

"I have loved you with an everlasting love."
Jeremiah 31:3

Time Out

• What is unconditional love? Read I Corinthians 13.
List some of the ways God expresses His love for you.

• What "bad thing" did the woman in John 8:3-11 do?
What was Jesus' response? What bad things did David do
in II Samuel 11? Did God cease to love David?

• Read Romans 8:38, 39. What is able to separate you
from God's love?

A Noble Calling

*I*f you work full time outside the home, I have some important information I want to share with you. But it doesn't come until the last half of this chapter. Can I ask you to skip down to the "Who Am I?" section and begin reading there?

If you stay home full time with your children, I need your immediate and undivided attention. Lock yourself in the bathroom. Set your alarm for 4 A.M. Do whatever you have to do in order to read these words uninterrupted.

You have a tough job. No pay raises. No annual reviews. No bonuses. No paid vacations. No health benefits. No fancy title.

Like Rodney Dangerfield, you have every reason to cry, "I get no respect."

Remember the last social you attended? The lady beside you introduced herself as Sylvia. "I own a catering business," she said. "What do you do?"

"I stay home with my three small children."

Sylvia gasped, looked past you, and said, "Excuse me, I see someone important I need to talk to."

Understandably, you were miffed. You wanted to grab Sylvia by the hair and shout, "Just a minute, blondie! I am an interesting person. I have hobbies. I tell terrific jokes. Just because I stay home with my children doesn't mean we have nothing in common! I could tell you catering stories that would curdle your cottage cheese." (Catering to your kids has made you a bit of an expert on the subject.)

But, being the gracious person you are, you politely smiled and bid Sylvia adieu. She glided past you as if you were never there in the first place.

Sylvia's reaction was nothing new. You are accustomed to being treated as a non-person. It happened this morning at the grocery store.

In the middle of a discussion with the bagger about the merits of paper over plastic bags, the cashier interrupted. "What's your work number?" she demanded.

"My work number is the same as my home number," you replied evenly. Your body tensed, hoping what you knew would happen, wouldn't.

It did. The clerk's eyes glazed over as if she were in a trance. She stared blankly somewhere beyond you. You waved your hands in her face and yelled, "Yoo-hoo! I'm here! I'm a real, live, walking, talking person."

But she knew better.

You had no work number. Which means you don't work. Which means you don't pay social security tax. Which implies you have no social security number. Which means you don't exist.

Furthermore, because you don't exist, you don't get paid. Which means you have no money. Which means you can't afford the Huggies diapers in your cart.

Sadly, she is probably right about the Huggies. Staying home with your children demands financial sacrifice. But she is wrong about everything else.

Let me set the record straight.

You count. You are important. No job is more vital than the one you are doing. You may not have a pile of money in your bank account, but a pile of rewards awaits you in heaven.

I know. You are thinking, "If what I'm doing is so significant, if I am as valuable as you say, why don't I feel important?"

Perhaps it's because you don't really know *who you are.*

When I quit my job at a prestigious university to stay home with my daughter, I relinquished my title. I lost my sense of personal identity. I was Pete's wife, Amanda's mother. I thought my name was Mommy-I-Want. In the meaningless repetition of daily chores, I lost sight of who I was and God's purpose for my life.

Who Am I?

One day I got hold of a piece of paper that changed my life. The paper listed thirty-eight biblical statements that described who I am as a result of my relationship with Christ. For three months, I studied these statements.

The first identity statement was Matthew 5:13: "You are the salt of the earth." Nice, but what did it mean?

I considered the attributes of salt. Salt stimulates thirst. Adds flavor. It is a necessary component for life. A preservative. It is valuable (salt was often used as money in Old Testament times). Salt purifies (it was rubbed on newborns during Jesus' day as a sterilizer).

As my list of attributes grew, so did my understanding. As salt, I stimulate in others a thirst for Christ. I am a preservative for good, a purifier in an evil world. Just by being myself, I add zip and flavor to life! "You are the salt of the earth." That's more than a nice thought. That's who I am!

The second statement from Matthew 5:14, "You are the light of the world," was equally enlightening (forgive the pun). Light. Where would we be without it? (In the dark!) Light makes vision possible. It allows us to see where we are going. Light is bright, warm, inviting. Light disperses darkness and evil. (If you don't think so, go to my old apartment in Dallas, turn on the light in the middle of the night, and watch the cockroaches run.) Light heals. Light causes growth. Light fortifies against depression. Light reflects.

As light, I illumine the way for my children. My bright spirit attracts others to the Lord. I seek to reflect Jesus in all I do. "I am the light of the world." Just saying it makes me stand a little taller.

Each identity statement gently turned the focus knob on who I was until, one day, the image became clear. I looked in the mirror and saw myself as God saw me: dearly loved; a joint heir with Jesus; a holy, blameless saint. (It's God who calls me a saint; I'm merely quoting Him!)

You are these things too if you have accepted Jesus as your Savior. Do you see yourself as God sees you? Are you convinced of your significance? your purpose?

Friend, hear me. Do not dismiss what I say as a "warm fuzzy" that momentarily makes you feel good. I am talking about who you are. This is something you must answer. You will never find real peace until you do.

Allow truth to sink in. Seek to know in the depths of your soul who you are in Christ. Grab hold of how much God loves you and claim His glorious plan for your life.

Jesus said He came that we might have life and have it abundantly (John 10:10). He didn't say, "I have come that your lives might be really mediocre."

Don't settle for less than abundant life. It is found in Jesus, by knowing who you are in Him.

Time Out

• Refer to the "Who I Am" statements in the appendix of this book. The first identity statement says, "I am God's child." What does it mean to be a child? What does it mean to have God as your Father? Is there anything a child can do to keep from being his father's child? How does being a child of God change the way you see yourself?

• Take one week to expound upon each identity statement. Memorize the statements and references that are the most meaningful to you. As you do this, ask yourself, "Which is more important, who I am or what I do?"

• Was Jesus' identity ever challenged? (Read Matthew 4:3-11; Mark 8:27-29; John 7:25-29.) Why was it crucial for Jesus to understand who He was and God's purpose for His life? What do you think would have happened if Jesus had lost sight of His identity or purpose?

Time Out
Truths

"Amanda, go to your room right now for a Time Out!" I commanded. "And don't come out until you can apologize to your sister for tying her up with the jump rope."

Amanda stomped off to her bedroom. I didn't know who was more frustrated, she or I. This was her fourth Time Out today. But it was good for her, I reasoned. Time Out gave her a break in the action. A chance to think things over. A chance to change her attitude.

I knew someone else who could use a Time Out.

I could!

The morning had started well enough. I hummed a song and thought, "It's going to be a great day." Then *whap!* The first confrontation between the girls knocked the song off my lips. *Pow!* The second squabble slugged the patience out of my intentions. *Whoosh!* The third storm sucked the joy from my spirit. By fight number four, lying unconscious on the floor seemed more desirable than playing referee. In a matter of hours, I'd gone from being hopeful to hateful.

I hate being a mother! I hate my kids' behavior! I hate my attitude!

That evening as Peter entered the house, I stomped out. "I'm taking a Time Out," I growled. "I'll be back after the girls graduate from high school."

True, I was filled with frustration. But I was also filled with determination. I *would* change my attitude. And I would not return until I had.

As the door slammed behind me, I knew I'd taken an important first step; I'd left my world (house, husband, and kids) and entered God's world (nature). The contrast was startling. I'd exchanged sibling arguments for singing birds. Mountains of laundry for mountains of majesty. The heat of the stove for the glow of the setting sun. Yes! A change of scenery was just what I needed to begin a change of attitude.

Inhaling deeply, I drank fragrant smells into my soul. Freshly cut grass. Sweet jasmine. Pungent pine. Quite a turnabout from a stinky diaper pail!

As I walked, I ordered my mind to block out the unhappy episodes of the day and dwell, instead, on God. First, I focused on *God's character.* I thanked Him for His patience. *Step.* His forgiveness. *Step, step.* His righteousness, holiness, and goodness. *Step, step, step.*

Next I praised God for *His works.* For healing Jan's cancer and Judy's broken heart. For giving Mark a new job, Tammy and Dave a new baby, and Vicki a new life.

I thanked Him for *His blessings.* A caring husband. Two healthy children. Cars that worked (most of the time), a roof over our heads, food at our table.

Earlier, my praise had been artificial, stiff. Now life flowed from it.

O great and Holy God, You alone are worthy of praise! I see Your touch everywhere I turn. You are in the beauty of changing seasons, in the wonder of changing hearts. The heavens declare Your splendor, the whole earth is filled with Your glory.

Forgive me, Father, for losing sight of Your glory. Help me see my child's endless questions as opportunities to tell her about You. Give me an attitude of thankfulness as I wipe spit up off the floor. Teach me patience as I pick up toys. Lift me above my circumstances and into Your joy.

A picture popped into my head, something my friend JoAnn had shared with me. "Sometimes I feel like a little girl in a big crowd. People are everywhere, pressing in on me. There's a parade, but I can't see. All I see are knees! I tug on my Father's pant leg and say, 'Please Daddy. Lift me up so I can see.'"

I was that little girl sitting on her Daddy's shoulders, high above my circumstances. Joyfully I praised God for parading His glory before me.

What a change! I had begun my Time Out fussing and whining. But along the way, God turned my complaints into praise. "You bestow glory on me and lift up my head" (Psalm 3:3).

I could almost hear God chuckle, **Aren't you glad you took Time Out with Me?**

As I mounted the steps to our home, I wrote three truths on my heart for future reference.

Truth Number One: Like my children, I require Time Out for attitude adjustment.

Truth Number Two: Joy is a choice. I choose it when I look to God, rather than to my circumstances.

Truth Number Three: Proper perspective comes as you sit on the shoulders of God.

I opened the door. Amanda rushed towards me and hugged me as if I'd been gone for a week.

"Mommy, Mommy!" she cried. "I missed you!"

My walk had only taken twenty minutes, but what a nice Time Out it had been!

"Your attitude should be the same as that of Christ Jesus."
Philippians 2:5

Time Out

• Do you consider Time Out for yourself to be a selfish or a necessary thing? When you take a Time Out, how do you spend it? Do you focus on God or do you go to the mall?

• Read Genesis 2:2; Exodus 34:21; and Psalm 62:5. God created the world in six days. On the seventh day, He rested. Why did God command the Israelites to follow His example and set aside one day a week for worship and rest? Why do you think God made this a command rather than a suggestion? Does the verse allow special circumstances to interrupt the rest?

• Isaiah 40:31 says, "Those who hope in the LORD will renew their strength. They will run and not grow weary, they will walk and not be faint." Rewrite this promise in your own words, using your own name and circumstances. How can this verse encourage you when you are unable to take time for a Time Out?

A Lesson from Dusty

"*I* love you."

Don't you love being loved? Think you could ever grow tired of hearing someone say, "I love you"?

Sometimes I hear an "I love you" in the sing-songy voice of my three year old. Other times I hear the words in the deep, masculine voice of my husband. Many times the words are from God.

God loves me. I am confident of it.

He loves you, too. Are *you* confident of it?

A friend recently told me, "I believe God loves me, but I don't *feel* loved. I know the truth in my head, but I am not experiencing it in my heart."

Ever felt that way? I have. The problem, I discovered, was *not* with my head or my heart, but with my ears! Over and over, God was saying, "I love you!" but I didn't hear Him because I was a lazy listener. Then one day I learned a lesson on listening from a dog.

Dusty nuzzled her furry face under my hand, pleading for a pat. Suddenly, she tensed. Every hair on her body stood at attention. Every muscle tightened. Her ears pricked forward, straining to hear. . . . *Whoosh!* Off she ran after a rabbit.

I hadn't heard the rabbit, but I wasn't exactly *listening* for one either. *That's why I'm not hearing God,* I thought. *I'm not listening—like Dusty—with my whole being.*

Once I put effort into my listening and fine-tuned the

ears of my spirit, I began to hear God. And hear God . . . and hear God.

I felt a little silly. All day long, God had been talking to me. Like Jacob, I shook my head in dismay and said, "Surely the LORD is in this place and I was not aware of it" (Gen. 28:16).

How did God talk to me? What did He say? As I watched the sun rise, awed by its unfolding beauty, He whispered, "I love you." An hour later He repeated "I love you" through a good-morning hug from my daughter. In the afternoon, He shouted "I love you" through the warm autumn sun and the kiss of the crisp, cool breeze. He told me a dozen times in a dozen different ways. A car that worked. "I love you!" An encouraging letter from a friend. "I love you!" An unexpected check in the mail. "I love you!"

Hearing God's voice is the first step in knowing God loves you. The second step is believing. You've got to believe God loves you even when your emotions tell you otherwise.

"For a long time, I'd based God's love for me on my *feelings*," my friend Lara said. "If I felt all 'ooey-gooey' inside, I knew God loved me. If the feelings weren't there, His love seemed distant, unreachable. Now I'm beginning to see that God's love for me is something deep and permanent, and that the emotions could very likely be a bad case of hormones."

Real love is lightyears beyond ooey-gooey feelings. When Pete and I were engaged, I had enough *ooey-gooey* feelings to fill a romance novel! Now, approaching fifteen years of marriage, ooey gooey would be a tragically shallow description of what I feel for Pete. Our love is solid, steadfast, unlike the temporal nature of fickle feelings.

My love for God has followed a similar course. When I

was sixteen, I fell in love with Jesus, all starry-eyed to learn that the mighty God of the universe loved little ol' me. A year later, my passion cooled. I'd pick a fight with God and stomp away in anger if I didn't get my way. In my youthful immaturity, my love for God ebbed and flowed like the tide. But His love for me was as constant as the pounding sea. Now, twenty years later, I am confident of God's love. I trust Him. He's never let me down. He will never leave me. And He will always love me . . . even when my emotions deny it.

Today I am struggling with my emotions. It's my birthday. Part of me says, *Today is a day like any other day. Don't expect anything special.* But another part of me wants a parade and fireworks. I want someone, meaning *everyone,* to make a big deal of the fact that I was born. I want a party with balloons and banners and a chocolate cake lit with candles. I want all the people I care about in one big room shouting, "We love you, Lorraine!"

I know. It's vain and childish. But I need to know that I am loved, that my life counts for something, that I am making a difference! Is that so much to ask? Out of the whole year, just one day on which the people I love say they love me?

No. One day is *not* too much to ask. In God's eyes it's too little to ask. God wants every day to be my "birth" day. He wants to greet me each morning with a kiss that says, "Today is your day. See the sun? I set it on fire for you. Look at the clouds. I parade them before you. The birds sing 'Happy Birthday.' All day long, in the heavens and on earth, listen to Me say, 'I LOVE YOU.' "

Regardless of how you feel at this moment, regardless of what has happened between you and God in the past, He wants you to know: He loves you.

People will forget to tell you they love you. They'll

even forget your birthday. Forgive them. Look instead to your heavenly Father, who whispers continually, "I love you."

Can you hear Him?

> *"I pray that you, being rooted and established in love, may have power . . . to grasp how wide and long and high and deep is the love of Christ, and to know this love that surpasses knowledge—that you may be filled to the measure of all the fullness of God."*
> *Ephesians 3:17-19*

Time Out

• During the last week, how has God told you He loves you? How are you aware of God's moment-by-moment presence in your life?

• Do you demand that "ooey-gooey" feelings accompany God's love for you? How can you push forward in your faith even when you don't feel like it? What is the connection between love and obedience?

• What are the characteristics of a good listener? Read Deuteronomy 30:20 and John 10:27. What do these verses emphasize? Why does James 1:19 admonish us to be *quick* to listen and slow to speak?

High
Hopes

*I*f ever a mother had high hopes for her son, it was Mary. When God arranges a miraculous conception, a birth heralded by angels, and visitation by royalty, something big is in the works.

As Jesus kicked within Mary's womb, she knew her child was destined for the greatest greatness. Set apart to lead a nation. Called to deliver God's own people.

Chosen for . . . a cross?

As Mary gazed from the foot of a cross toward her beaten, dying son, what did she feel?

Anger? Of course! Her innocent son, humble and loving, hung on the nails of other people's sin. Righteousness suffered at the hands of the guilty. Good crucified while evil walked free. Such injustice was an outrage!

Agony? Certainly! Her heart broke over her own inability to comfort her firstborn during His hour of greatest need. She longed to wipe the blood from His feet, to put cold cloths on His swollen eyes and to gently clean the gouges in His back where the whip had slashed His skin. As His collapsing lungs gasped for air, her own breath became a curse to her, a reminder that while life flowed through her, it flowed out of her dying son.

But the emotion Mary felt most strongly, the emotion that pulled her to her knees and ripped through her soul, was despair. Cruel, hateful despair that smashed her dreams, shattered her faith, and left her screaming in silent darkness, "Why?"

Why, God? Why did You allow this to happen to Your beloved? Why didn't You stop Pilate before he pronounced the sentence? You sent fire from heaven to save Elijah and consume the prophets of Baal. Couldn't You have done the same to save Your own Son?

Why, God? You told Isaiah to announce His coming. You sent an angel to proclaim He would be a king. You said He'd sit upon the throne of David, that He would reign forever. Why did you promise these things if they were never to be?

Why did you give Him power to heal the sick? to scatter demons? to raise the dead? Why did You stir up a nation through Him only to let Him die?

When He was two years old, You snatched Him from the jaws of death. For what? For this? For a cross?

A picture flashed through Mary's mind. Three days earlier she had watched as the people lined the road at the Mount of Olives, joyfully praising God, waving palm branches as Jesus rode into Jerusalem on a donkey. "Hosanna!" they shouted. "Blessed is the king of Israel" (John 12:13).

Mary was certain, then, that Jesus would come into His kingdom. But the people turned on Him. Shouts of "Hosanna" became cries of "Crucify Him!" Rather than Jesus leading the Jews, the Jews had led Him . . . to Golgotha. Instead of raising Him to a throne, they had lifted Him on a cross.

"King of the Jews" mocked the sign above His head. Mary longed to rip it down, to throw it at the sneering crowd and scream "Look what you've done to my son!"

Instead, she slumped at the cross and wept. It was too late. Her son would die. Jesus would never be king. The people had lost their Savior.

God had failed.

Or had He?

We have an advantage over Mary. We know the end of her story. We understand how, even though it seemed impossible, God would fulfill His promises to her.

Knowing this, wouldn't you love to step back in time and comfort Mary at the foot of the cross? Wouldn't you love to put your arm around her and whisper, "Don't cry, Mary! It's going to be okay. No grave can hold your son. He *will* be king. God *hasn't* let you down. Be patient; you will see. God is about to surpass all you've ever dared to hope or dream!"

God has an advantage over you, too. He knows the end of *your* story. He already knows how you will get through the thing in front of you.

Can I put my arm around you and whisper something in your ear? "Don't despair! God will not fail you. He has a plan. Be patient; you will see. God intends to do something in you and through you that will surpass all you've ever dared to hope or dream."

Our God is mighty. Bigger than anything facing you. Trust Him. Trust in His high hopes for you. He says, "For I am going to do something in your days that you would not believe, even if you were told" (Hab. 1:5).

"With man this is impossible,
but with God all things are possible."
Matthew 19:26

Time Out

• Like Mary, are you struggling with a situation you don't understand? Are you able to trust God even though it seems hopeless?

• True or False: If I love God and study His Word, I should always understand His actions. For the correct answer, read Isaiah 55:8, 9 and Romans 11:33-36.

• As a parent, you often choose not to explain yourself to your children because their young minds cannot comprehend your reasoning. When this happens, how do you want your children to respond? How does God want us to respond when we are unable to understand His ways?

Read It Again, Mom!

"*R*ead!" Megan commanded. She shoved a book into my hand and wiggled up next to me on the couch.

I glimpsed the familiar orange-and-green cover. *Oh, no. Not* Goodnight, Moon*!* During the raising of our two daughters, I calculated reading the book no less than one zillion times.

Megan snuggled closer, expectantly. Forcing myself into my "good mother role," I flipped back the cover. No need to look at the words. I knew them by heart.

"In the great green house . . ."[1]

Megan clapped her hands with delight, anticipating the cow jumping over the moon and the three little bears sitting on chairs.

I turned a tattered page. The copyright date on the book was 1947. A friend, who had read the story to her four children when they were young, had passed the book on to me when I was pregnant with Amanda. One day I would pass it on to my children to read to their children—if it held together that long! I smiled as I visualized Linda reading it to her family more than thirty years ago. Did she know, then, that her actions would be repeated in future generations?

"Mommy! Look! I found the itty-bitty mouse!" Megan shouted triumphantly, as if she'd discovered it for the first time.

Why is this book always new to you, Megan? Trying to

comprehend her excitement, I studied my daughter as I continued. "Goodnight room, goodnight moon, goodnight light and the red balloon . . ."

Megan pointed to the balloon.

"What other things in the picture are red, Megan?" I asked.

She pointed to the red flames in the fireplace. The red bowl full of mush. The red carpet.

A red light went on inside my head. *Stop, Lorraine. Think for a few moments and you will understand why Megan loves this book.*

I remembered Megan at six months. Then, what she enjoyed most about *Goodnight, Moon* was not the story, but the sound of my voice and the rustle of turning pages. When she was one, she liked to find the itty-bitty mouse that appeared throughout the book. At eighteen months, colors were her concern. Now, approaching three, she was preoccupied with finding the letter *O*.

As if reading my thoughts, she shouted, "There's an *O!*"

Then I understood. *In the comfort of familiar words and pictures, Megan ventures out, joyfully making new discoveries.*

Take Megan's enthusiasm for *Goodnight, Moon*, double it, and you get an idea how I feel about the Bible.

I never tire of reading it. In the comfort of familiar words and pictures, I make new discoveries. I come across a verse I've read many times and marvel, "Wow! I never saw that before." I hear a sermon on the very passage I studied the night before and wonder, "How did I miss *that* insight?"

The Bible has a great beginning (in the beginning God created . . . and it was good) and a great ending (the beauty of heaven and the triumphant return of Christ). Pages in between contain drama, suspense, mystery, romance, poetry, and passion, all woven into a riveting plot only God could conceive.

No book compares with the Bible. What other writing claims to be flawless (II Sam. 22:31)? to have the power of life and death in its words (Deut. 30:15, 16, 19, 20)? to provide direction, wisdom, and truth (Prov. 2:6-11)?

The psalmist declares, "I meditate on your precepts and consider your ways. I delight in your decrees; I will not neglect your word" (Psalm 119:15, 16).

I don't want to neglect God's Word, but two demanding preschoolers make uninterrupted reading a challenge. Sometimes I grab one minute and find one verse I want to memorize. I write it on the bottom of my grocery list. Each time I add an item to my list, I repeat the verse. Even during an exceptionally hectic week, I can memorize one verse. Often, it's that very verse that gives me the strength or encouragement I need to get through my day.

On other occasions God and I get more time together, but it never seems like enough. *You say Your Word is "living and active,"*[2] I remind God. *Time is short. Please, make Your Word come alive to me!*

I play a little game that helps. I pretend the words on the page are actually alive. "Okay, guys," I challenge them. "What do you have to say to me today?" Like a roomful of toddlers waking up from a nap, the words squirm, stretch, then jump into action.

"Look at me!" shouts one verse. "Watch what I can do," boasts a paragraph. Several words on the opposite page holler, "Over here! You've got to see this!"

Other times I imagine the Word of God to be a tall glass of water. With each swallow, the cool liquid seeps into the dry areas of my soul, refreshing me. Once I have drunk deeply and my thirst is satisfied, my spirit bubbles forth, creating an overflow from which others can drink. I bear testimony to the truth of Jesus' words: "Everyone who drinks this water [earthly water] will be thirsty again, but whoever drinks the water I give him [spiritual water] will never thirst. Indeed, the water I give him will become in him a spring of water welling up to eternal life" (John 4:13).

I love God's Word! But, I confess, I haven't always felt this way. I remember times I yawned my way through the New Testament, bored out of my mind. *I'm not getting anything out of this,* I'd think. *Why am I wasting my time?* But I kept reading out of allegiance to some Sunday-school mandate that proclaimed daily Bible reading as a necessary ingredient for all good Christians. I read the words, but they never reached my heart.

What changed? What ignited my passion for the Word?

Jesus.

I know now that Christianity is not about *religion.* It is about a *relationship*—a very intimate relationship with Jesus Christ.

"Jesus loves me! this I know, For the Bible tells me so."[3] It's one thing to sing the childhood song. It's another thing to experience it. From Genesis to Revelation, the Bible shouts of Jesus' love for me. *Me!*

Being in love, and having someone love you in return, changes everything about you. Just ask the teenager with the goofy grin on her face and her boyfriend's class ring on her finger. She'll tell you. Being in love is wonderful. You cannot stop talking about the object of your affection. You replay his words in your mind. You read his love letters again and again.

The Bible is God's love letter to me. Jesus is my lover. I was sentenced to die, but my lover courageously died in my place. One day we'll be together. Until then, I read and reread His letters. I pore over them, continually surprised to discover new things about the One I thought I knew so well. As I read, I sense Him beside me, pointing out things He wants me to know. His letters are my most precious possession. I weep that someone loves me so much.

One day I hope to know each page of the Bible as well as I know each page of *Goodnight, Moon.* After I finish reading to Megan, she always asks, "Can we read it again?" Wouldn't it be great if we felt that way about God's Word?

> *"Take to heart all the words I have*
> *solemnly declared to you this day . . . .*
> *They are not just idle words for you—they are your life."*
> *Deuteronomy 32:46, 47*

Time Out

• On a scale of one to ten, one being "not intimate" and ten being "very intimate," how would you rate your relationship with Christ? How does intimacy between two people develop? What can you do to enjoy closer fellowship with Jesus?

• If Christianity is enjoying a personal relationship with Jesus, why is so much emphasis placed on "Christian disciplines" (reading Scripture, praying, memorizing verses, going to church, etc.)? In which area do you most need to grow: the *disciplines* or your *personal relationship with Christ?* What can you do to encourage your development?

• Read Psalm 119. See if you can find nineteen benefits to knowing the Word of God. Memorize Joshua 1:8. How can Scripture memory help you do what this verse suggests?

[1]Margaret Wise Brown, *Goodnight, Moon* (Clement Hurd: Harper & Row, 1947). Used by permission of the publisher.

[2]Hebrews 12:4.

[3]Anna Bartlett Warner, "Jesus Loves Me," 1860.

Off-the-Wall Conversation

"*I* really hated to see them go," Paint sighed.

"So did I," Wallpaper agreed. "It's awfully quiet in here with Amanda and Megan gone."

"Know what I will miss?" Paint asked.

"No," Wallpaper said.

"Those wonderful wall rubs their mother gave me when she wiped away the crayon scribbles and sticky handprints. So relaxing. . . . Did wonders for my stress marks. What will you miss, Wallpaper?"

Wallpaper thought for a moment, then replied, "I will miss not seeing the children grow up. I spent all my time hanging around the crib. One minute Amanda was a baby; the next she was a confident little preschooler. I was looking forward to watching Megan grow up, too. It's hard to see her go after only two months together! Oh, well. I guess it wasn't meant to be . . ."

"I still can't believe they moved," Paint remarked. "Can you imagine hauling that tiny little baby half-way across the country! She was so sweet, so precious, so . . ."

"Whiny!" snapped a voice below.

Paint and Wallpaper were floored that Carpet dared invade their private conversation.

"No one asked you, Carpet," Paint sniffed.

"I'm glad those spoiled troublemakers are out of here," Carpet snarled.

Paint brushed the comment aside, but Wallpaper,

normally the more composed of the two, came unglued.

"Spoiled troublemakers! How can you be so cruel?" Wallpaper accused.

"Me? Cruel? Those rug rats were the cruel ones. They drooled all over me, soaked my pad with milk, and wore me to a thread," Carpet complained. "And their noise! 'Good-bye and good riddance' is what I say! Now maybe we can have some peace and quiet around here."

"That's the problem," Paint moaned. "It's *too* quiet. When Amanda and Megan left, they took the laughter with them."

"Laughter, hah!" Carpet mocked. "All they ever did was cry. Cry for food. Cry for a diaper change. Cry for Mama. Nothing but wall-to-wall crying for three years."

Paint turned red with anger. "I *know* you're a carpet, but how can you lie like that! Amanda and Megan filled this room with sounds of love."

"Now Paint, don't lose your tempera," cautioned Wallpaper, who by now had regained his composure. "It's all a difference of opinion. Carpet contends that the girls filled this room with sounds of crying. Paint and I allege that the children filled the room with sounds of love."

"That about covers it. And if Ceiling were awake, I'm sure he would be on my side," Carpet said boastfully.

"Don't be ridiculous. He's *above* such arguments," Paint fumed.

"Now Paint, don't get stirred up," Wallpaper cautioned. "Let's restrain emotion and examine the facts." Then, like a seasoned trial lawyer, Wallpaper pleaded their case. "I intend to show beyond all reasonable doubt that for three years Amanda and Megan filled this room with the sounds of love. I call on Carpet as my first witness."

"You're crazy," Carpet said indignantly.

"Tell me, then. What caused those two long, narrow

dents in your fibers near the closet?"

"You know perfectly well that that is where that creaky rocker sat. What are you getting at?"

"Carpet, do you recall what happened on the morning of April 24, 1988, when Amanda woke for her 3 A.M. feeding?"

"Sure do. The kid woke up screaming. Bawling her eyes out. Just proves my point. She was a crybaby," Carpet gloated.

"But," Wallpaper interjected, "when the mother heard Amanda's cries, she came in, settled with her in the rocker, and sang to her while she nursed her."

"That's right, Carpet," Paint chipped in. "There was singing. Lots of singing."

Wallpaper continued. "Remember when Amanda was one year old and she came down with bronchitis?"

"Do I!" Carpet said. "She cried nonstop for weeks . . ."

"And for weeks, the mother and father prayed over her as they rocked with her in the chair."

"That's right, Carpet," Paint said excitedly. "There was praying. Lots of praying!"

Wallpaper was on a roll. "And remember last Saturday just before bedtime? Amanda, her mother, and Megan rocked back and forth in the old rocker. And what did they do while they rocked?"

"They laughed!" Paint shouted. "There was laughing, Carpet. Lots of laughing."

Then, a pause. As the three roommates privately reminisced, sounds of love echoed off the empty walls of the nursery.

"I guess those girls weren't so bad," Carpet admitted. He waited to hear "I told you so." Instead there was a long silence.

"It *is* kinda quiet in here," Carpet sighed.

"Not for long," Paint said cheerfully. "You know the family that's moving in next week? I understand they have triplets!"

"My house shall be called a house of prayer."
Matthew 21:13

Time Out

• If the walls in your house could talk, what would they say? Which concerns you more: how your home looks or what goes on inside of it?

• Wallpaper said that praying, laughing, and singing were evidence of love in the home. Determine one activity in each of these areas that you would like to do with your family in the next week. Examples: 1) We will have a family prayer time on Sunday evening; 2) We will rent a funny movie and watch it together on Saturday night; 3) Each night before bedtime we will sing "Jesus Loves Me."

• In this story, Wallpaper was a peace-keeper. Read Romans 12:14-21. According to this passage, what can you do to keep peace in your home?

A Balloon
for Julia

*T*he pink balloon floated heavenward. A string dangling from the balloon carried a message for Julia: *Are you having fun playing in the clouds?*

Julia was two when she died. In her short life she suffered much—holes drilled into her skull and four open-heart surgeries—but she also loved much and brought joy to many.

"Julia was a happy child," her mother, Noelle, recalls. "She loved music. I remember sitting with her at the piano. She'd bang the keys, then bounce up and down excitedly as if she'd played some great masterpiece. And she loved going places. When someone was about to leave the house, she'd scoot across the floor on her bottom to the front closet, pull out her cap, and point to the door. She wasn't about to be left behind!"

Unfortunately, many of Julia's outings were trips to the hospital. Born with a heart disease and a detached pulmonary artery, life for Julia became a series of surgeries. Following one operation, blood accumulated in her brain, causing her to become deaf and blind.

For four weeks, Julia lay unconscious. Noelle and her husband, Paul, used the long hours to write Bible verses on 3 x 5 cards which they taped to Julia's bed. Friends added their favorite verses. Noelle smiles as she recalls Julia's card-covered bed. "Many people were encouraged by those Scriptures. Julia was unconscious, but that didn't stop God from using her!"

As Julia rested on God's promises, healing flowed through her frail body. Four weeks later she opened her eyes. Her vision and hearing returned.

But the family's trials were not over. Clots formed in Julia's artificial heart valve. Back to the hospital for more surgeries and the installation of a pacemaker.

"It was one complication after another," Noelle sighs. "I kept telling myself, 'Lord, Julia is Yours. I know You have a plan in all this.'"

It soon became clear to Paul and Noelle that God's plan included bringing Julia to heaven to live with Him. As God gently prepared the parents for Julia's departure, they prepared their daughter. Each night, as Paul tucked Julia in bed, he asked, "Honey, is God building a mansion in heaven for you?" Julia would look up, smile, and clap her hands excitedly.

Six months passed. Then one morning, Noelle awoke with the unmistakable thought, *Today Julia's suffering will end.*

"Julia was in such pain," Noelle recalls. "Her body was in a state of dehydration. I picked her up and held her in my arms. She was doing a 'death groan,' huffing and puffing like a locomotive. Gradually her breathing slowed. Sixty breaths a minute. Ten breaths a minute. Three. Then nothing.

"She lay on my lap, still. I kissed her good-bye. Julia was with Jesus." Through tears, Paul and Noelle sang over their child's motionless body "Great Is Thy Faithfulness."

At the memorial service, a pink balloon floated heavenward, carrying a message to Julia from her family. A program with Julia's picture on it carried Julia's message to those she loved: "My flesh and my heart may fail, but God is the strength of my heart and my portion forever" (Psalm 73:26).

"I miss Julia." Noelle says. "I think of her every day. I know I'll see her again."

Second Corinthians 4:14, 16, 17 promises this: "We know that the one who raised the Lord Jesus from the dead will also raise us with Jesus and present us with you in his presence. . . . Therefore we do not lose heart. Though outwardly we are wasting away, yet inwardly we are being renewed day by day. For our light and momentary troubles are achieving for us an eternal glory that far outweighs them all."

There is a notion among some Christians that, because they believe in God, God should somehow spare them from suffering. The Bible clearly refutes this. "Dear friends, do not be surprised at the painful trial you are suffering as though something strange were happening to you" (I Peter 4:12). "In this world you will have trouble" (John 16:33).

God never promised to spare us from suffering. He promised instead to walk with us in our suffering and to encourage us by revealing His glory in the future and His goodness in the present.

Noelle found great comfort in Psalm 27:13: "I would have despaired unless I had believed that I would see the goodness of the LORD in the land of the living" (New American Standard Bible).

Paul and Noelle saw God's goodness in the present through friends who lovingly wrote notes, brought meals, and helped pay medical bills. They will see God's glory in the future when they enter heaven's gates and are greeted by a smiling child holding a pink balloon.

"I consider that our present sufferings are not worth comparing with the glory that will be revealed in us."
Romans 8:18

Time Out

• Do you know someone who is suffering? What did Noelle's friends do to encourage her? Ask God to show you how you can minister to your friend in need. (Warning: While the promises of God can be of great comfort, as they were for Noelle, not every person struggling with grief will see it this way. Handing someone a Bible verse should never be viewed as a quick-fix for deep suffering.)

• First Peter 2:21 says, "To this you were called, because Christ suffered for you, leaving you an example, that you should follow in his steps." What does this mean? Why did God allow Jesus to suffer, even though He could have prevented it? What does suffering produce in us? (See Romans 5:3.)

• Do mud marks on your freshly waxed floor or crayon marks on the wall cause you to grumble? Think of Noelle who would welcome these sights. The next time you find yourself frustrated by your child, stop and hug him. Then praise God for the life with which you have been entrusted.

• Buy your child a balloon and attach a love note to it.

Author's Note: Paul and Noelle have begun a grief ministry to encourage parents who are suffering a loss. As of the printing of this book, God has blessed them with a son named Clark.

The Unorthodox Oreo

*I*t was the most unusual cookie I had ever seen. It couldn't be dunked in a glass of cold milk or twisted apart like the sandwich cookies from my childhood.

Round, black, and four feet in diameter, this Oreo had a painted smile, swinging arms, and fast-moving feet.

I spotted it tap dancing by the potato chips in aisle six.

White-gloved hands motioned for my two year old to come closer.

"Look, Amanda," I said. "The cookie is waving at you." Beside the cookie, a red-haired lady passed out miniature counterparts of the towering, tapping treat.

Amanda stared. Her mouth dropped open. I thought she wanted a cookie.

"Whaaaaa!"

I was wrong. Her wail shook the Pepsi display. Amanda grabbed my neck, screamed in my ear, and buried herself in my coat. A flash of brilliant maternal reasoning caused me to conclude that she was scared out of her diapers. I wheeled the cart in the opposite direction, towards Deli. Meanwhile, heads peered over canned goods to see if I were abusing my child.

I could handle this. Mothers faced these kinds of crises every day. As usual, food was the solution. I stuffed crackers in Amanda's mouth so she couldn't scream, then devised a strategy for gathering my groceries without going into the domain of the dreaded dancing cookie.

"Close your eyes, honey. Mommy is going to take you on a ride."

I popped a wheelie and slid safely into aisle five, nearly upending an old man toting a sack of dog food. Amanda seemed delighted, but the man with the Kibbles didn't look too happy.

Ten minutes later, I smugly crossed off the last item on my list. Mission accomplished. All cookie contact had been successfully avoided. I headed for the check-out, dismissing the nagging feeling that I had forgotten something.

As we approached the cash register, I groaned. The animated Oreo could be seen from every single check-out lane. *Oh well, a mother's got to do what a mother's got to do.* I grabbed a balloon on a stick and stuck it in Amanda's face. This worked for about thirty seconds; then she saw through my ruse.

Like a repeating air-raid siren, Amanda sounded her alarm. The check-out clerk winced. "Didn't get a nap today, huh?"

"No," I sighed. "And I need one. I've got a headache."

On one hand I sympathized with Amanda. *Poor Girl. I don't blame you for being afraid of that big, scary thing with the flapping arms!* On the other hand, I was frustrated with her. *For goodness sakes, child! Lighten up! It's just some kid dressed in a cookie costume.* Unfortunately, neither of these responses would help Amanda understand what she really needed to know: her fears were groundless. There was no need to be afraid.

We all have our dancing cookies. My sister-in-law is terrified of flying. David fears losing his job. I am afraid we won't have enough money to send our children to college.

Do you think our fears ever frustrate God?

Wild waves unmercifully pounded the fishing boat. "Lord, save us! We're going to drown!" the disciples cried. "You of little faith, why are you so afraid?" Jesus asked and calmed the sea (Matt. 8:26). The crowd told Jairus, "Don't bother Jesus. Your daughter is dead." Grief filled the ruler's eyes. "Don't be afraid," Jesus said, and He raised Jairus's daughter from the dead (Mark 5:35-42). Peter eagerly walked toward Jesus on the water until he saw the wind and began to sink. "Lord, save me!" Peter pleaded. Jesus pulled Peter from the sea and sighed, "Why did you doubt?" (Matt. 14:29-31).

"O unbelieving and perverse generation . . . how long shall I stay with you and put up with you?" Jesus asked in Luke 9:41. At times, the groundless fears of His followers frustrated Jesus. If only they could see what He saw—nothing was impossible. One nod from God and the sun would stand still, food would fall from the sky, the lame would walk.

But fear blinded the people. Like sheep without a shepherd, they skittishly flitted about, fleeing imaginary predators. As Jesus looked into their fear-filled eyes, frustration gave way to compassion. "Do not be afraid, little flock," He tenderly encouraged (Luke 12:32). "Do not let your hearts be troubled" (John 14:27).

Jesus consoled His followers. He urged them not to fear people or circumstances. "I tell you, my friends, do not be afraid of those who kill the body and after that can do no more. But I will show you whom you should fear: Fear him who, after the killing of the body, has power to throw you into hell. Yes, I tell you, fear him" (Luke 12:4, 5).

Jesus taught His disciples what they should—and should not—fear. He also taught them how to conquer fear.

"Jesus took with him Peter, James and John the brother of James, and led them up a high mountain by themselves. There he was transfigured before them. His face shone like the sun, and his clothes became as white as the light. Just then there appeared before them Moses and Elijah, talking with Jesus. . . . A bright cloud enveloped them, and a voice from the cloud said, 'This is my Son, whom I love. . . .'"

"The disciples . . . fell facedown to the ground, terrified. But Jesus came and touched them. 'Get up,' he said. 'Don't be afraid.' When they looked up, *they saw no one except Jesus*" (Matt. 17:1-8, emphasis mine).

The four-point plan for conquering fear is this: Get facedown on the ground. Let Jesus touch you. Release the fear. Then look up and see *only* Jesus. Keep your eyes on Jesus and you will know what He knows: there is nothing to fear.

Oh, by the way. Remember that nagging thought that I was forgetting something at the grocery store? I did.

Cookies.

"Be strong and courageous. Do not be afraid or terrified . . .
for the Lord your God goes with you; he will
never leave you nor forsake you."
Deuteronomy 31:6

Time Out

• List two of your fears. What are the reasons behind these fears? Try to see your fears through the eyes of an all-powerful, all-knowing God. How do they look?

• Read II Kings 6:8-18. An army was sent to capture Elisha and his servant. Elisha was calm. His servant was afraid. Why? What did God show Elisha's servant that caused His fear to vanish?

• "The LORD is my light and my salvation, whom shall I fear?" (Psalm 27:1) "The one who is in you is greater than the one who is in the world" (I John 4:4). "Perfect love drives out fear" (I John 4:18). Pick one of these verses and memorize it. Then, next time you are afraid, focus on God's truth—the Scripture you memorized—rather than your fear.

Word Watch

*T*he missionary's report was sobering.

A little girl, five years old, climbed the hill because she wanted the purple orchid as a gift for her mother.

"Don't go off the path!" her mother had warned. But the child couldn't help herself. In such desolate surroundings, the flower's beauty drew her like a magnet.

She grabbed the stem and pulled.

BOOM!

The blast hurled her small frame through the air like a rag doll. Moments later, when she opened her eyes, she gasped. With the orchid, her hand and foot had been blown to bits.

Officials estimate that more than 30 million land mines were scattered throughout Afghanistan following Russia's invasion in 1979. The United Nations and other peace-keeping organizations work around the clock to disable the mines, but all too often the mines do their own disabling first.

Afghanistan is a country of the walking wounded. Pictures show a man with no legs. A child with a stump of a hand. A mother bound with gauze and supported by the aid of a crutch. They fill the public places, their wounds visible to all.

America, too, is a land of the walking wounded, but unlike the Afghans, we hide our wounds. A bomb explodes. We act as if nothing happened. We ignore the cries of pain. We pretend we do not see the broken hearts and emotional limps.

The Afghans' injuries are the result of explosives packed in steel casings. Our injuries are the result of anger packed in words.

I know what you are thinking. *That's crazy, Lorraine! How can you compare words to bombs? Aren't you being a bit . . . overly dramatic?*

Maybe.

Maybe not.

Proverbs 18:21 says, "The tongue has the power of life and death." Anyone want to chide King Solomon for being overly dramatic?

James describes the tongue as a fire burning wildly out of control (James 3:5-6). Surely a raging fire can do just as much damage as a bomb.

Women are particularly susceptible to tongue tirades. It starts when we are young. Little boys fight with fists. Little girls fight with words. Even as we mature and discover more appropriate ways to express our anger, we must always resist that inner temptation to drop a bomb.

"What a slob! Just look at your room." *BOOM!*

"I've told you a thousand times not to do that. What is wrong with you?" *BOOM!*

"Why can't you be more like your sister?" *BOOM!*

And then there's the atom bomb, the Big One dropped too many times in too many homes. The one your child fears each time you and your husband argue.

"Your father is impossible to live with. We're getting a divorce." *KABOOOOM!* The child's world is blown apart. An ominous cloud hangs over him, and he is never the same.

Peter and I are committed to the success of the family.

That's why we started a marriage ministry. But every once in a while, we bump into a couple whose marriage seems hopeless.

Lord, I can't bear to see this family destroyed! What can I do?

Pray, He urges. **Pray that the husband and wife will turn to Me because I alone can put the pieces back together. And,** He continues, **do all you can to protect your own home from becoming a war zone.**

As a wife and mother, *what* I say impacts my home. But *how much* I say is equally important.

"When there are many words, transgression is unavoidable, but he who restrains his lips is wise" (Prov. 10:19, NASB). Translation: Know when to close your mouth.

"The more the words, the less the meaning; and how does that profit anyone?" (Ecc. 6:11) Translation: Know when to close your mouth.

"But I tell you that men will have to give account on the day of judgment for every careless word they have spoken" (Matt. 12:36). Translation: Know when to close your mouth.

Well, I don't have to be told twice! (Not when three times will do.)

But closing my mouth isn't easy. So I sought help.

Psalm 141:3 says, "Set a guard over my mouth, O LORD; keep watch over the door of my lips."

Seeing the wisdom in this, I hired a mouth guard. Two, in fact. Sensitive, sensible Boris (who champions love) occupies the right side of my mouth. Burly, brave Brutus (who champions truth) occupies the left.

Here's how my mouth guards work; A word wells up within my heart and pushes its way up my throat. As it comes to the door of my lips, Boris and Brutus cross their swords, halting the word. After a quick inspection, if the word is edifying, my guards uncross their swords and let it out. But if it's critical or hurtful, they promptly march the word back down my throat.

I can't tell you how many times I've gagged on my words with such force that some kind soul has rushed to get me a glass of water.

My faithful mouth guards have prevented me from blasting others, but occasionally I've let my guard down and allowed hasty words to escape. When this happens, I rush to the workshop of my mind and locate two tools.

Tool One: "I'm sorry. I was wrong."

Tool Two: "Will you forgive me?"

It's amazing how, when properly used, these two tools can defuse even the deadliest bombs.

> Before you drop your next word bomb
> Here is something you should think on.
> Words can hurt or they can heal,
> When you've been bombed, how do you feel?
> Instead of wounding, please forgive,
> It's a much more pleasant way to live.

"Do not let any unwholesome talk come out of your mouths, but only what is helpful for building others up according to their needs, that it may benefit those who listen."
Ephesians 4:29

Time Out

• Hire your own mouth guards. Personalize them by giving each a name. Write a job description that includes character traits you desire in your guards as well as specific job responsibilities. Place the job description in your Bible next to Psalm 141:3.

• Read Proverbs 10, and list the positive and negative characteristics associated with the tongue. Be sure to look up any cross references associated with these verses.

• Have you dropped any bombs lately? Contact someone you have injured and apologize.

• Attach a smell to each of your words. Positive words smell like freshly baked cinnamon rolls; negative words are dead fish; neutral words are broccoli (which is only offensive if it boils too long). Describe what people smell when they walk into your home.

A Good
Name

Some parents give little thought to the names they give their children.

"I scanned the credits at the end of a movie and picked out the name I liked best."

"My husband suggested we name the baby Gilbert and I thought, *Why not?*"

"Our son will be named after his father, who was named after his father. That's how it's done in his family— that way the monogrammed towels can be passed down from one generation to the next."

Other parents invest endless hours determining an appropriate name for their offspring.

"We took the first two letters of my father-in-law's name, the first three letters of my mom's name, added an extra *n* and finally came up with a name we agreed upon."

"The baby is due next week. We've narrowed it to forty-two girl names and fifteen boy names."

Many parents choose a name from a "baby name" book. Somewhere between *Aaron* and *Zelda* is *Ichabod*.

I'd never call my child *Ichabod* (people would probably shorten it to *Icky*) because *Ichabod* means "the glory of the Lord has departed."

The wife of an Israelite priest named her child *Ichabod* after she learned that the Philistines had captured the ark of God, God's holy throne on earth (I Sam. 4:19-21). Understandably the theft upset the woman. But it saddens me that in her anger she gave her child a bad name.

Think about it. The baby wears an ID bracelet at birth that says, "The Glory of the Lord Has Departed." The lad is at school. His teacher takes roll call. "Your name, young man?" He stands and announces, "The Glory of the Lord Has Departed." On his wedding day, his wife looks at him and pleads, "Honey, can we use my name instead of yours?"

A child's identity is tied to his name. Poor Ichabod. At the mention of his name, smiles vanished. Brows furrowed with sorrow. Shoulders sagged with sadness. All because one person chose to give another a bad name.

Name-calling is a serious business. Isn't it sad that we treat it so lightly?

Mrs. Smith marches overactive Tommy to the principal's office and reprimands, "You are a Troublemaker." A mother at the grocery store glares at the broken jar on the floor and scolds her child, "How could you be so Stupid!" A little girl stuffs a handful of popcorn into her mouth at the theater. Her father growls, "Don't be such a Pig."

Last week at a church social, I overheard several parents discussing their children. "Jim's real smart," bragged one father. "A first-class athlete, too. But his older brother is a Bum. Never will amount to anything."

What names do you call your children? When my girls behave, I utter endearments like *Honey Buns, Pumpkin Pie* and *Sweet Cakes* (I have a mild food fixation). But when they disobey, their names aren't so sweet.

One day Amanda took my red lipstick and scribbled all over the 100-year-old quilt hand-stitched by my great-great-grandmother. As I labored unsuccessfully to remove the stains, I muttered, "Child, you can be so Exasperating!" Amanda did not understand the meaning of the word, but she cried anyway because she knew

Mommy had called her a bad name.

The childhood rhyme, "sticks and stones can break my bones, but names can never hurt me," is a lie. Names *do* hurt. I've seen more than one person destroyed by ugly labels slapped on her identity. This grieves God. He intended for names to say something positive about who a person is, or what that person would become. For example, *Abraham* means "father of a multitude." God called *David* "a man after My heart." His name means "beloved." *Jesus* means "salvation."

God has many names. Each name describes some aspect of God's character. *Elohim*, used over 2,700 times in the Bible, means "One Who Is Great, Mighty, Dreadful." *El Shaddai*, which occurs 48 times in the Old Testament, means "Almighty." *El Roi* means, "The One Who Sees." *Jehovah-Jireh*, "I Am Provider." *Jehovah-Rophe*, "I Am Healer." *Jehovah-Nissi*, "I Am the Standard." *Jehovah-M'Kaddesh*, "I Am the One Who Makes You Holy." *Jehovah-Shalom*, "I Am Peace." *Jehovah-Rohi*, "I Am Shepherd." *Jehovah-Tsidkenu*, "I Am Righteousness." *Jehovah-Shammah*, "I Am in You."

Aren't the names of God encouraging? Don't you wish, like God, you had a fistful of encouraging names to describe you?

You do.

When you were born, your parents chose several names for you and recorded them on a birth certificate. When you were "born again" by accepting Jesus as your Savior, your heavenly Father chose more than thirty names for you which He recorded in the Bible.

Your new names include *Chosen*,[1] *Dearly Loved*,[2] and *Friend*.[3] God christened you *Saint*,[4] *Holy and Righteous*,[5] an *Ambassador*,[6] as you act as *Salt*,[7] and *Light*,[8] to a needy world. You are a *Joint Heir with Jesus*,[9] a *Child of the King*,[10] a *Member of a Royal Priesthood*.[11]

Do you embrace your Christian names? Or do you still allow negative childhood names like *Stupid, Fatso,* or *Failure* to describe you?

Release those old names. They don't belong to you. Satan would love to render you ineffective by getting you to believe his lies rather than God's truth. Don't do it!

Instead, accept your new identity as a child of God. The experts say you will live up (or down) to the names you are given. Aren't you grateful that God has given you such noble names?

"A good name is more desirable than great riches."
Proverbs 22:1

Time Out

• What names do you call your children? What names do you call yourself? Does your thinking align with biblical truth?

• Review the "Who Am I?" statements in the appendix. What names are most meaningful to you? Why?

• Make a list of the names of God. Beside each name, describe a situation where God proved to be who He said He was. Example: "God showed Himself to be Jehovah-Jireh, I Am Provider, by giving me a place to live when I had no money."

[1] Colossians 3:12.
[2] Colossians 3:12.

3 John 15:15.

4 Ephesians 1:1; Philippians 1:1.

5 Ephesians 4:24.

6 II Corinthians 5:18-20.

7 Matthew 5:13.

8 Matthew 5:14.

9 Romans 8:17.

10 I John 3:1, 2.

11 I Peter 2:9, 10.

Section Three: I'm a Big Kid Now

"*L*et us leave the elementary teachings about Christ

and go on to maturity." —*Hebrews 6:1*

The Most Important Question

*T*here were no windows or doors in the room. The white walls, ceiling, and floor generated an incandescent light. The room was empty except for the chair on which I was sitting and the unusual man in front of me.

His long hair and flowing robes were the purest white. His eyes were two gentle flames, warm and inviting, like soothing candlelight. He appeared to float rather than stand.

He listened to my confessions.

"I did not boil my baby's pacifiers for the full five minutes as instructed on the package. I stole my daughter's M & M's when she wasn't looking. I spanked in anger . . ."

"Wait," the man commanded. "You do not need to tell me these things. They are already written down."

The man raised his hand. Suddenly three people appeared in the room, each carrying a seven-foot-tall stack of paper. While I was trying to figure out how they had gotten into the doorless room, they set the stacks in front of me and vanished. I stood on my chair, peeked over the paper mountains, and called to the man in the white robes.

"What are these?"

"Your sins."

Impossible! These couldn't be my sins! Sure, there had been times I'd yelled at the kids, times I'd fallen short in my "Christian duty" to others. But overall I was a good mother. A good person. I taught my children to pray and sing worship songs. I attended church regularly. I brought meals to people in need. I even led Bible studies!

"You led Bible studies," said the man, reading my thoughts. "Surely you recall Jesus' words in Matthew 12:36—'I tell you that men will have to give account on the day of judgment for every careless word they have spoken.' "

I never liked that verse. . . . Still, there had to be some mistake. These were someone else's sins, not mine! I grabbed a few papers off one of the stacks and began to read. Even though the records were written in a foreign language, I could understand them.

Driving Sins

May 14, 1990, between 4:30 and 4:45 P.M.

Items: Illegal U-turn, exceeding speed limit, throwing candy wrapper out the window, telling Amanda to shut up, and calling a fellow driver a crude name.

I dug deeper.

Lies

April 7, 1991.

Items: "I don't have time to read my Bible." "I'll pray for you, Susie." "It's not wrong as long as no one gets hurt."

With each account, a video played in my mind, rewinding me to the moment of my sin.

I was guilty. Back then, my sins had not seemed so serious. But here in the white room they were black, vile.

I dropped the papers and hung my head.

Tenderly, the man touched my shoulder.

"You also remember, do you not, that there is no condemnation for those who are in Christ Jesus."

"Yes," I sobbed. *But why had I put Jesus through the agony of the cross because I was careless about what I said and did? Why hadn't I taken my sins seriously?*

"I must go," the man said. "There is Another with whom you must speak. He will ask you the Most Important Question."

In a blink, he disappeared, leaving me alone with my sins.

What happened next cannot be described within the confines of words. But you must try to glimpse the glory. You must try to comprehend that you, too, will one day face the Lord.

A warm breeze blew through the room. In the distance, a trumpet sounded. Suddenly a brilliant, white light exploded around me. Terrified, I fell to the floor on my face. My hands covered my eyes, but I could not shut out the brilliance of the light.

Then I heard a voice that sounded like a thousand rushing rivers. In the midst of my holy fear, my heart rejoiced, for I knew the voice.

It was my Savior.

"Lorraine."

"Yes, Lord."

"Look at me."

His glory so great, my huddled frame so small. In frightened obedience I lifted my head and looked into the burning face of the Son of Man. Out of His mouth came a sharp, double-edged sword, and in His right hand were seven stars.[1] He looked into my soul and asked the Most Important Question.

"Did you love Me with all your heart, soul, and strength?"

My body shook. My lips trembled. I could utter no sound in the presence of His kingly splendor.

But hidden in the glory was Someone familiar.

My comforter and companion, Jesus.

I had met Jesus through a high school classmate who

shared how Jesus had become her best friend, how He had delivered her from drugs and despair. Through her testimony, He became my best friend, too. Every morning Jesus sat with me and explained the Scriptures. Throughout the day we talked. We laughed and cried. We worked side by side. Ever faithful, ever caring, Jesus. I had never known a truer friend.

I looked into the face of the Son of Man. At that moment, I was grateful that the fullness of His majesty had been hidden from me on earth, or I never would have dared to draw so near.

He waited patiently for an answer to His question.

"Lord, You, more than anyone, know how much I loved You." I thought of the paper mountains. "But You also know how often I failed You."

"Lorraine, remember when we met? You believed then that I would take care of your failures. Do you believe that now?" He repeated, "Do you love Me?"

"Lord, You know I do."

He smiled. "That is all I ever asked, little lamb."

He pointed to my sins. Three silver pitchers appeared above the paper stacks. Slowly, they tipped, pouring forth rivers of blood which covered my sins and melted them into nothingness. Jesus pulled me close. I wept with relief in the arms of my Savior.

When I opened my eyes, I knew this had been no ordinary dream. God had momentarily pulled back the curtains to the future, allowing me to glimpse that which would be.

The morning sun streamed through the window. My shower could wait. I had something more important to do. I knelt by my bed, folded my hands and prayed, *Dear Jesus, thank You for taking care of my sins. I love You. With all my heart, soul, and mind, I love You.*

*"Jesus replied: ' "Love the Lord your God with all
your heart and with all your soul and with all your mind."
This is the first and greatest commandment.' "*
Matthew 22:37, 38

Time Out

• In Luke 14:26, Jesus said, "If anyone comes to me and does not hate his father and mother, his wife and children, his brothers and sisters—yes, even his own life—he cannot be my disciple." Why does Jesus say we are to hate those we love? What does He mean?

• How strong is your love for Jesus? List anything you love more than Jesus (spouse, kids, talents, pleasures, health, your life). Ask God to make your love for the Savior the greatest passion of your life.

• Do you take your sins seriously? Spend a few moments worshiping the Lord for His holiness. Thank God for giving you a Savior to cover your sin so you can enjoy moment-by-moment fellowship with Him.

• Read I Corinthians 3:11-15. Today is your Judgment Day. Scenes from your life flash before you. What is your response? What is God's response? The "fire" has just burned through your life. What remains?

[1]Revelation 1:13-17.

Author's Note: This chapter describes a dream. I don't intend to communicate that these are actual Judgment Day events or that salvation happens apart from believing in Jesus Christ and accepting His death on the cross as payment for your sins.

What Am I—
Your Servant?

"More jews! More jews!"

Amanda was not announcing a population explosion in Israel. She was demanding her favorite drink.

I shuffled to the refrigerator and retrieved the pitcher of apple juice.

Lack of sleep blurred my vision. I missed the cup by several inches. I had so many bags under my eyes I felt like an ad for Samsonite luggage. During the night, I'd gotten up three times to nurse the baby and once to find "Spot," who had fallen to the floor out of Amanda's reach.

I snapped the sippee lid on the cup and handed it to my daughter.

"Kicks! Kicks!" she demanded, pounding the tray of her high chair.

I glared at her for a moment, debating how to respond to her request.

"Kicks, please!" she corrected herself.

I trudged back through the kitchen and grabbed the cereal box. As I poured Kix into Amanda's bowl, I heard Megan crying in the other room. *Feeding time already?* I moaned. Something warm trickled down the front of my nightgown. My stomach rumbled. My own hunger would have to wait. I had two other mouths to feed.

As I shuffled in the direction of Megan's cries, I tried to recall my life before children.

What was it like to eat a meal sitting down? How did it

feel to sleep through the night? to go to the bathroom without an audience?

How would it be to have only *myself* to dress? to smell like perfume instead of diaper wipes? to wear a blouse free of drool marks?

I longed to read a book uninterrupted, to look through a window and see the backyard rather than jelly handprints, to lie on the couch without getting impaled by a Lego.

A satisfied *coo* interrupted my thoughts. Megan nursed contentedly. She was so cute. As she sucked, her nose wiggled up and down like a bunny's.

I rubbed her soft, fuzzy head and smiled. I did not resent my children for the way my life was. In fact, I was grateful to them. My children had shown me something about myself I never would have learned any other way: I am selfish. Not just sorta selfish, but *really* selfish.

Before having children, I did not acknowledge my self-centeredness. After all, I did nice things for my husband, helped my co-workers with their struggles, and volunteered at church. But any serving I did was because I *chose* to serve at a time that was convenient for me. When my children were born, my ability to choose died. I was thrust into the role of on-call servant, like it or not.

Much of the time, I didn't.

I stomped around the house, picked up toys, made beds, folded laundry, and growled at my husband and children, "What *am* I, your servant?"

They ignored my complaints. God didn't.

Yes, Lorraine, He affirmed. You *are* their servant.

Great! I wanted a little sympathy, a little help, a little cooperation. Instead, I got conviction.

I've never found servanthood very appealing. When asked what I wanted to be when I grew up, I never once said, "I want to be a servant."

Yet Jesus says we should all aspire to be servants. "If anyone wants to be first, he must be the very last, and the servant of all" (Mark 9:35).

Because I want to obey Jesus, I want to serve. But it's not easy! Too often I end up in a vicious tug of war with my will. The fledgling servant in me wants to tell my husband, "Go play racquetball, honey. You've had a tough week and the exercise will do you good." But the sinful me snaps, "What do you *mean*, you want to play racquetball?! All week you go to a clean, quiet office, while I'm stuck in a messy house with loud, demanding children. I'm the one who should go to the gym! The only exercise I had this week was sixty knee bends with a laundry basket."

Selfishness is ugly. Fortunately, God is teaching me something beautiful through Galatians 2:20: "I have been crucified with Christ and I no longer live, but Christ lives in me."

That helps. When I am unable to find it within my heart to serve, I order my sinful nature to sit in "Time Out" and let *Christ in me* serve in my place. When I want to look at a magazine, but my kids want me to make Play-Doh worms, my selfish self goes to Time Out and Jesus in me molds the dough. When I want to go for a walk, but my husband wants to play racquetball, Jesus in me packs Pete's gym bag. When I am hungry, but my children want to be fed *now,* Jesus in me makes the peanut butter sandwiches.

Jesus' life was a life of service. He said, "For even the Son of Man did not come to be served, but to serve" (Mark 10:45). He asked others, "What do you want me to do for you?" (Mark 10:36, 51). He never demanded His rights. He often postponed personal desires so He could minister to others. In the end, He even gave His life for those He loved.

And yet, Jesus did not serve others to the point of neglecting His own physical and spiritual needs. He took time to eat and rest. He regularly withdrew from the crowds. He understood the need to be "filled up" in order to give out.

One of Jesus' last acts of servanthood was to wash the feet of His disciples. Inspired by His actions, I purchased a special foot-washing pan and some fragrant cream. Then, one night when my husband came home from a particularly bad day at work, I washed his feet.

It is difficult to explain what happened between us as I rubbed his swollen arches and massaged his toes. As I looked up into his face, I saw a curious mix of emotions. He seemed honored, yet humbled, that I would do this for him. Then our eyes locked, and something happened. The invisible bond between us strengthened. Until that moment, I had always believed that serving was about obedience. Now I knew it was also about love.

I have much to learn about being a servant. Daily I ask God to help me die to self and live for others, to serve as unto the Lord. As I pray, I am discovering that God is not only doing something *through me*, He is doing something *in me*. He is making me more like Jesus.

So, thank you, children. Were it not for you, I'm not sure I would ever have learned what it truly means to put others before myself.

> "*Be very careful . . . to love the Lord your God,*
> *to walk in all his ways, to obey his commands,*
> *to hold fast to him and to serve him with*
> *all your heart and all your soul.*"
> *Joshua 22:5*

Time Out

• In your own words, define the word *servant.* Make a list of ten adjectives you feel best describe a servant.

• Do others see you as a servant? How can you become more comfortable in this role? How does God's view of a servant differ from the world's view of a servant?

• What are some attitudes that can prevent you from effectively serving others? How can these attitudes be changed? What is your motive for serving? What was Jesus' motive? (Read John 6:38.)

Homecoming

*J*ack pulled a box from the truck and walked toward the shabby two-bedroom house. Cars zoomed behind him on the busy city street. He studied the sagging roof and tiny dirt yard. He hated moving his wife, four children and two pets here. But Jack had no choice.

The house his family had rented for the past two years had sold. This was the only place they could afford. The landlord waived the security deposit with the understanding that the family would clean up a few things left by the former occupants. The "few things" included drug paraphernalia, pornographic magazines, crusty fast-food boxes, and furniture and clothes unfit for Goodwill.

For two weeks the family hauled out trash, scrubbed floors and fixed holes in the walls. But mostly, they prayed. Even after the garbage was gone, an oppressive spirit lingered. "Daddy, are you *really* going to make us live here?" cried his daughter Shannon.

Jack took four-year-old Kerry with him to load up the last of their belongings at their former home. Finally, the rooms were empty. All that remained were memories. They had grown so close as a family here! Reluctantly, Jack locked the front door for the final time.

"Say goodbye to the house, Kerry," Jack said as he backed down the driveway. Kerry looked troubled.

"I wanna go home, Daddy," Kerry said, tears filling his eyes. "But where *is* home?"

Have you ever felt like Kerry? Unsettled? insecure? longing for a home but uncertain where "home" is?

Abraham did. For years he and his family wandered through deserts and strange cities in search of a place that God would give him. He longed for a better country—a heavenly one.

Moses dreamed of a home. He was an alien in Egypt. Convinced his home lay elsewhere, he packed his bags and spent the next forty years in search of a better land.

Christ, too, longed for His home. For thirty-three years Jesus purposefully carried out His Father's work. He loved the people. He loved the land. Still, Earth was not His home.

One day Jesus gathered His disciples around Him. You can almost hear the excitement in His voice, see the twinkle of anticipation in His eyes. "My kingdom is not of this world," He said (John 18:36). "I came from the Father and entered the world; now I am leaving the world and going back to the Father" (John 16:28).

As Jesus spoke, questions stirred in the hearts of His disciples. *Why, Jesus? Why are You leaving?*

"In my Father's house are many rooms. . . . I am going there to prepare a place for you" (John 14:2).

For me? You mean I am coming to live with You? But I thought this was my home.

"If you belonged to the world, it would love you as its own. As it is, *you do not belong to the world,* but I have chosen you out of the world" (John 15:19, emphasis mine).

So, You are saying I don't belong here. I belong with You. And You are fixing up a place for me. What will it be like?

"No eye has seen, no ear has heard, no mind has conceived what God has prepared for those who love him" (I Cor. 2:9).

In heaven, there is a city of gold, brilliant and clear as

crystal. A street of gold runs through it. Around the city is a great, high wall made of jasper. In the wall are twelve gates, each gate is a single pearl. The city shines with the glory of God. There is no need of the sun or moon to shine on it, for the glory of God gives it light and the Lamb is its lamp. (See Revelation 21.)

"The dwelling of God is with men, and he will live with them. They will be his people, and God himself will be with them and be their God. He will wipe every tear from their eyes. There will be no more death or mourning or crying or pain" (Rev. 21:3, 4).

Can you imagine the disciples' excitement as they heard about heaven? "Sounds beautiful. I can't wait to see it!" "I'll be glad to be free from the constant pain in my knee." "Never again will I have to bury someone I love."

In heaven you will *never* hear:

> "Your mortgage is due."
> "Sorry. We can't use you."
> "Stop worrying."
> "The doctor says it's hopeless."
> "Your child has just been in an accident."
> "What you are asking is impossible."

You *will* hear:

> "Holy, holy, holy is the Lord God Almighty."
> "Wow!"
> "How wonderful to see you again."
> "It sure feels good to be home."

On Earth, you will always feel a bit restless. This is not your home. *Heaven* is your home. Ponder its existence. Long for it. "Set your mind on things above, not on earthly things" (Col. 3:2). Remember, "our citizenship is in heaven. And we eagerly await a Savior from there, the Lord Jesus Christ" (Phil. 3:20).

Lord Jesus, I can't wait to see You in the fullness of Your glory! Keep working on that mansion. One day, I'll see it. One day, I'll be home.

*"There is surely a future hope for you,
and your hope will not be cut off."*
Proverbs 23:18

Time Out

• Are you certain you are going to heaven? How can you be sure? (See I John 5:11-13.)

• In Romans 12:1, Paul urges us not to be conformed to this world. What are some ways you might conform to the world? How can you set your eyes on heavenly purposes rather than on earthly pleasures?

• Usually it is not the place but the people that make a house a home. Who will be in heaven with you? Who will be absent? Ask God to bring to mind those who need to hear about the hope of eternal life and to give you the courage to share Jesus with them.

• Read I John 2:15 and James 4:4. What is "friendship with the world"? Why does James call us *adulterous* if we are friends with the world?

Amanda's Grace

"I AM SICK OF THIS, DO YOU HEAR ME?" I screamed. Amanda trembled. Of course she heard me. The *neighbors* heard me. She burst into tears and ran for the safety of her bedroom.

Tears trickled down my cheeks.

What kind of mother am I? Why am I hysterical over a few scribbles on the wall?

The intensity of my anger startled me. I felt like a failure. Defeated, I slumped to the kitchen floor and wept. I cursed the out-of-control hormones poisoning my emotions. I condemned myself for inexcusable anger. I blamed Amanda for disobeying. How many times had I warned her not to use the walls as her personal art canvas? For once, couldn't she mind me?

The writing on the wall had set off my explosion, but for days it had been fueled by the constant whining, the arguing, the push . . . push . . . pushing at my patience until I could take no more. I had a right to be angry! Didn't I?

No. Even as I sat on the linoleum crying, I was convicted that nothing justified yelling at my child with the ferocity of a bear caught in a trap.

I would have to apologize, explain that sometimes Mommy acts a little crazy. (My "wacko wacko"[1] times had intensified since Megan's birth. Would our family survive until I reached menopause?)

I opened the door to Amanda's bedroom. Immediately she hugged my knees, eager to mend the rift between us.

"Sorry, Mommy," she repented. "I won't write on the walls ever again."

I kneeled on the floor and gathered her in my arms.

"I forgive you, Honey. I did something wrong, too. I shouldn't have yelled at you." My voice choked. "Will you forgive me?"

"Yes, Mom. And Jesus forgives you, too," she said matter-of-factly.

The incident was quickly forgotten in Amanda's mind, but not in mine. Guilt hopped on my right shoulder. Condemnation perched on the left. Both sunk their claws into my flesh and whispered repeatedly in my ear, "You are a terrible mother."

During the next few days I proved their accusation true as I continued to blow it with my kids. I was short, jumpy. I cut off innocent questions with a snap. I passed out "don't mess with me" glares as freely as a Las Vegas dealer passes out cards. I slammed snacks in front of their apprehensive faces and kicked toys out of the living room.

A few times I checked my behavior, but the winds of rage returned the instant my orders were not met with prompt obedience.

For three days, my sense of failure immobilized me and caused havoc in our home. Guilt and Condemnation no longer whispered in my ear. Now they shouted: "YOU ARE A TERRIBLE MOTHER!" I had to shut those voices up. I had to make a change, and change, for me, always started with a heart-to-heart talk with God.

Problem was, God and I weren't speaking. I had purposely avoided Him, certain He didn't want to hear from the likes of me. I couldn't bring myself to approach a holy

God feeling this dirty. So I did what I always do when I feel really bad. I took a bath.

Tears slid down my face and plopped into the water, sending rings of ripples across the surface.

God, forgive me for being so horrible to my children! I've let them down. I've let You down. I am such a failure.

I was sure God would agree with me. Condemn me. Spank this naughty child of His with a lightning bolt. Lord knows I deserved it!

He did none of this. Instead, He comforted me.

Lorraine, you are not a failure. As He spoke, He reached for Guilt and Condemnation, intending to remove them, but after three days on their perch, they'd grown quite comfortable. They were not about to leave without a fight. Resolutely, they dug their claws deeper into my flesh.

But God, I yelled at my kids. I've been crabby, mean, and impatient. I've thought of no one but myself.

This was silly. Why was I arguing with God? Why was I trying to convince Him that I was a failure? Surely He could see that for Himself.

Lorraine, He persisted, **you failed. But you are not a failure. Do you see the difference?**

A weight lifted from my shoulders.

I soaked in the water of God's grace for several more minutes, floating on the forgiveness He so freely offered. The warmth and wetness soothed me, purified me. I put the soap back in the dish and reached for a towel. I was clean.

Why is it so difficult to forgive ourselves when we fail? Perhaps it is because God has embedded within us a sense of justice, an intuitive understanding that wrongs must be righted, evil must be punished. God knows, if we were disciplined immediately for every sin we committed, we'd be nothing but a black-and-blue lump of flesh! So He started a better plan. He introduced Jesus. He instituted grace.

Why grace? Not because we deserve it, but because we need it. Grace frees us from guilt and condemnation. Grace liberates us from the prison of sin. Grace elevates us to a higher level of living.

One more thing: Grace is best entered into quickly. Hebrews 12:15 says, "See to it that no one misses the grace of God and that no bitter root grows up to cause trouble and defile many." For three days, I had allowed a bitter root to grow in the soil of my heart. By the time the Lord—by His grace—pulled it out, it had grown into a four-foot weed. It was easy to see how unchecked bitterness can grow to the size of a tree, requiring a crew of experts to remove it.

I'm sorry I hesitated to enter God's grace; but I'm glad that Amanda embraced it immediately. In a way, that was fitting. Amanda's middle name is *Grace*, in honor of her great-grandmother Grace Lee. Perhaps *Grace* should be my middle name, too!

> *"Let us then approach the throne of grace with confidence, so that we may receive mercy and find grace to help us in our time of need."*
> *Hebrews 4:16*

Time Out

• When you fail, do you find it difficult to forgive yourself? If God proclaims that there is no condemnation for those who are in Christ (Rom. 8:1), why do you condemn yourself? Why does God say that grace must be received by faith?

• Look up definitions in the dictionary for *grace* and *forgiveness*. Why must grace and forgiveness go hand in hand? Can grace and forgiveness be earned? (See Ephesians 2:8.)

• Do you quickly extend grace and forgiveness to those around you? When you hesitate to do so, what is the result? (See Hebrews 12:15.)

[1]Let me thank Kit May for a nice way to describe the not-so-nice side effects of premenstrual syndrome.

Myth of the Perfect Parent

I'd like to take a stick of dynamite, shove it under the phrase *"perfect parent,"* and blow it to bits.

There is no such thing as a "perfect parent." "Perfect parents" are imaginary beings, created in the minds of writers, who appear in fiction books or on family TV shows.

They are not real. They do not exist.

Agree? Then I'm sure you *never* kick yourself for being less than perfect. After all, it makes no sense to punish yourself for not living up to something that doesn't exist! Right?

Face it. Like me, you scold yourself when you blow it with your kids, because, in a moment of weakness, you buy into the lie of the "perfect parent." You blame yourself for not being more like Karen, who spends ten-hour stretches with five preschoolers and still comes up smiling. Or Dave, who tells his boss he won't work on Saturday because he promised to take his kids to the zoo. Or Lisa, who home-schools five children, reuses sandwich bags, and bakes her own bread.

Who is on your "perfect parent" list? Write their names on a sheet of paper. Think about each person. I'll bet my stretch marks you really don't know even one "perfect parent," but rather a group of parents who collectively embody the notion of a "perfect parent."

Let me explain.

When it came to newborn nurturing, Jan was my "perfect parent." The instant Jan smelled a baby, her arm crooked into the shape of a cradle. I, on the other hand, feared babies, refusing to hold them lest I'd drop one and it would break. When Amanda was born, Jan patiently instructed me in my fumbling attempts to care for my child. I learned more by watching Jan and how she responded to my daughter than I ever learned from my bookcase brimming with parenting books.

Just when I got the "infant thing" down, Amanda became a toddler. It was like having a different person in the house. I called on another "perfect parent," Tammy. My easygoing, redheaded friend taught me the right songs to sing and directed me to age-appropriate resources. Parenting, as I learned through Tammy, was a delicate balance between discipline and love.

Then Amanda became a preschooler. (Would she *never* quit changing on me?) She begged me to play Red Rover and Barbies. Childhood games were as foreign to me as a French menu. I called on another "perfect parent," Kit, a kid in adult-size Nikes. Her eager curiosity and playful nature encouraged me to join in water balloon fights and jungle-gym acrobatics. Kit not only taught me how to play with my daughter, she awakened in me the childlike wonder I had abandoned at age seven when my father died and I had become an instant adult.

Jan, Tammy, and Kit each came into my life at the perfect time with exactly the help I needed. The combination of these three mothers became my "perfect parent." I hadn't intended to label my friends this way; it just happened because I kept comparing my parenting weaknesses to their parenting strengths. But comparing is unwise. When I compare myself with someone else, I either come up short or become puffed up with pride. Both alternatives are self-destructive.

Once I stopped comparing myself to my friends and accepted them for who they were—their strengths *and* weaknesses—I began to relax in my parenting. It was such a relief to realize I didn't have to excel in every aspect of mothering! Separately, my friends and I were far from perfect. But when we used our strengths to help each other, our parenting came a little closer to perfection.

In the movie *Rocky*, Sylvester Stallone describes his relationship with Adrian as, "I got gaps. She's got gaps. Together, we got no gaps."

That is a pretty good summation of II Corinthians 12. We all have gaps. That is why God designed the body of Christ to be interdependent. We desperately need each other's strengths and, yes, weaknesses.

God never intended us to parent in isolation. It saddens Him when we do so. And it saddens Him when we push another person up on the "perfect parent" pedestal just because they are gifted in an area we are not. (How would you like it up there—lonely, vulnerable, and destined to fall?)

Slapping a "perfect parent" label on anyone is an injustice to you and to the person you label. Now, don't you agree it's time to blow up the "perfect parent" label once and for all?

Good. Give me that "perfect parent" list you made earlier. I want to use it to light the fuse.

One . . . two . . . three . . . *KABOOM!*

"To all perfection I see a limit . . ."
Psalm 119:96

Time Out

• Read I Corinthians 12:1-30. Why do you think God designed the body of Christ to be interdependent? Are you reluctant to ask for help when you need it? Do you freely give help when help is needed? How does exercising a gift benefit the giver? the receiver?

• Invite several friends to your house for a "gift exchange." Give each person a sheet of paper and have each draw two columns. In column one, ask each to list her most pressing need. In column two, have each list talents or areas of strengths. Then mix and match as God leads!

• You are the product of imperfect parents. Does this ever hinder you from seeing God as a "perfect parent"? In what ways are your parents like God? In what ways are they different?

• During the last week, in what ways did you compare yourself to someone else? What was the result? Why do you think Paul tells us in II Corinthians 10:12 that we are foolish when we compare ourselves with others? What are some Bible verses that talk about your uniqueness?

Take My Advice

Some dictionaries define *mother* as a stringy, gummy, slimy substance formed by bacteria in vinegar. Certain days, this describes me pretty well. Other days, I embrace another definition of *mother*: a woman who has borne a child.

I find this second definition of *mother* incomplete. A true mother goes beyond bearing a child—she diligently and lovingly raises that child until he is grown!

Mothering is an exhausting, all-consuming process that requires energy, concentration, perseverance, patience, and a host of other elusive attributes. What mother has not wondered at some point in her parenting, "Will I ever make it to the day when my youngest is potty trained?"

I talked with nine parents who successfully survived the formative years of their children.

"If you could share one piece of advice to encourage mothers in the stresses of rearing preschoolers, what would it be?" I asked. Here are their responses.

Live one day at a time. Madalene Harris, mother of four, says, "Sometimes, it's good not to look too far down the road. For thirteen years I changed diapers. That thought overwhelmed me! But changing diapers for one day? I could handle that. Matthew 6:34 says, 'Do not worry about tomorrow, for tomorrow will worry about itself. Each day has enough trouble of its own.' When life was difficult I'd tell myself, 'Just get through today, Madalene.

Forget tomorrow.' That helped, not only when my children were young, but later when I lost my husband to cancer. I now know that it is best to live life one day at a time."

Don't be afraid to ask for help. "As much as you need help is as much as I need to give it," suggests Kit May, mother of three. "I love to help others. It's fun! We all need help. We all need to *be* helped. That's why God gave us to each other. John 16:24 says, 'Ask and you will receive, and your joy will be complete.' Never be afraid to ask someone to help you."

Keep your marriage a priority. First you have a husband, then you have kids. It's easy to forget the importance of that order when your children are little, says Sherron Hudson, mother of two adult children. "There were times I was so stressed out from my day that I dumped on John the minute he walked through the door. That didn't work. What *did* work was to make John my first priority. I began spending the last thirty minutes before he came home preparing for his arrival. I'd put the kids in their rooms for a quiet time, comb my hair, put on a clean blouse, splash on some perfume, and pick up the house. When John opened the door, I greeted him with a kiss. Over time, his attitude about coming home changed. He no longer worried that a challenge awaited him the minute he opened the door. Instead, as I was sensitive to meet his needs, he became eager to meet mine. The best thing I did for my children—and my marriage—was to honor John and put his needs first."

Keep your goals simple. Lauri Bumann, mother of three, remembers, "When my children were babies, I felt as though I accomplished nothing. Doug would ask me at dinner, 'What did you do today?' and I couldn't point to a thing! So instead of setting goals I'd never achieve, I set one or two *simple* goals. I'd take the kids on a walk and use that time to talk to God. This accomplished a spiritual goal and an exercise goal. I love to entertain. Instead of having friends over for a five-course meal, I'd invite them for dessert. Sometimes I'd think, 'Boy, that's not much.' But it was realistic! And it kept me moving in a positive direction."

Cherish each moment. John Davis, father of two teenagers, suggests, "Be glad that, right now, your kids want to be with you. In the snap of your fingers, they'll be gone. The other day I asked Jeff if he wanted to go to the movies with me. He said, 'No, Dad, I've already made plans to go with my friends.' It seems like yesterday that Jeff was four, tugging on my pants legs, begging me to play with him. Now I am the one doing the begging. None of us can return to those early years once they are gone. That is why it is so important to enjoy the moments while you have them."

Apply consistent discipline early on. One of the best ways to ensure future peace is to be willing to have a little conflict early on, says Pat Reger, speaker for MOPS (Mothers of Preschoolers). "I tell mothers, discipline your children when they are young if you want them to be responsible when they are adults. Be consistent. Think before you threaten. Then, follow through on what you say. Doing this now will prevent a lot of heartache in the future."

Hebrews 12:11 says, "No discipline seems pleasant at the time, but painful. Later on, however, it produces a harvest of righteousness and peace for those who have been trained by it."

Don't neglect your spiritual life. Phyllis Stanely regularly mentors mothers with young children. "For many women," she says, "mothering does not come naturally. But we can mother *supernaturally* if we rely on the power of the Holy Spirit. It is impossible to realize the power of the Holy Spirit without spending some time reading the Word of God and praying. Often I hear, 'I don't have time for God. Maybe when my kids are older. . . .' But the mother who can't find time for God when she has two toddlers won't find time for God when she has two teens. Begin *now* to develop your relationship with God. Make your kids have a quiet time so you can have your quiet time. Once you realize that you have nothing of lasting value to offer your children apart from what God gives you, spending time with Him will be your top priority."

Be willing to admit when you are wrong. Don Couchman, grandfather of three, offers this: "It's important to be humble and honest with your children. If you make a mistake, admit it. Your kids are smart. They will realize you are not perfect. As teenagers, they will be more likely to share their struggles with you and seek your counsel if you have been open in the past about your own failures."

Stay home with your kids. Susie Jernigan, mother of three: "There is a lot of pressure on mothers to work outside the home, but children need their parents with them, especially when they are little. Staying home means making personal and financial sacrifices, but in the long run, it's better than sacrificing your child. If at all possible, put work—and even ministry—on hold so you can cherish those sweet bonding times with your little ones. My home was and is my most important job. Anything that continually conflicts with that is out of God's will for me. I don't know what God's will is for your life. All I can do is encourage you to listen to Jesus. What is He telling you to do?"

There you have it. Advice salted with godly wisdom from nine seasoned parents. I have nine tips of my own to share, not nearly as profound, but useful nonetheless.

1. Buy stock in companies that produce bandages and diapers. You will feel a sense of elation at being personally responsible for the economic success of these firms.

2. For girls, never buy a dress without first considering the "twirl factor."

3. For boys, don't worry if the only word he knows is *vroom*. Before you know it, his vocabulary will expand from engine sounds to include body noises.

4. Don't throw away unused breast pads. They make terrific coasters.

5. Keep your sense of humor. What upsets you now will be good joke material in five years.

6. When your child wants to wear the same outfit two months in a row, let him. Eventually it will rot and fall off.

7. In all situations, apply the "Thousand Year Test." Ask yourself, "In a thousand years will anyone care?"

8. Don't be too hard on yourself. You will fail. Forgive yourself and move on.

9. Above all, love "because love covers over a multitude of sins" (I Peter 4:8).

> "*Plans fail for lack of counsel,*
> *but with many advisers they succeed.*"
> Proverbs 15:22

Time Out

• Go over this advice with a friend. Each of you pick one point you'd like to incorporate into your parenting. Share your intentions, and commit to call each other once a week to monitor your progress.

• Which more accurately describes you: "I need help," or "I am able to give help"? Ask God to show you what actions you need to take based on your circumstances.

• God encourages us to seek counsel from others but never at the exclusion of seeking counsel from Him. According to John 14:26, who is your daily Counselor? What kind of counsel does this person give? What situations in your life could benefit from His counsel?

I'm a Big Kid Now

After weeks of back-to-school specials, the day finally arrived.

Kathy's palms were sweaty. Her stomach churned. Would the teacher be nice? Would the kids be friendly? A purple backpack stuffed with school supplies lay by the front door. Ready. But Kathy was not ready. She felt like throwing up.

If this was how *she* felt, how must her five year old feel?

The first day of school often is more traumatic for parents than it is for the child. This was certainly true at our home.

Amanda and I began preparations for kindergarten weeks in advance. "These shoes are too small for you," I said. "We'll have to get a new pair before school starts. You are such a *big girl.*"

Even as I spoke, her legs seemed to lengthen another inch. So why was I surprised to find she had not only outgrown her shoes, but everything in her closet as well?

As I stacked crayons, shoes, and pants on the check-out stand at Wal-Mart, Amanda beamed at the clerk, "I'm going to school. I'm a *big girl* now."

The bus was due any minute. I studied my daughter. Did she understand that from this day forward, her life would be forever changed? She looked so grown up in her new outfit.

"You are such a *big girl,* Amanda," I said.

Suddenly, an enormous yellow monster with thirty eyes rumbled up the road. It stopped in front of us, opened its mouth, and sucked up my child. Then, with a burp of black smoke, it roared away, carrying my firstborn in its belly.

"No!" I cried. "She's so *little!*" In that moment I realized my "baby" was gone forever. I spent the next hour with a box of tissue.

My reaction surprised me. I thought I'd prepared us both for this day. But then, maybe a mother is never prepared for her child to grow up. Nevertheless, growing up is the bottom line of life. It is the goal of our children. It should be our goal as well. *But how can you know when you are all grown up?*

Under the stairs in the house where I was raised, there are pencil marks and dates scribbled on a wall to record the growth of each child in our family. I remember standing on my tiptoes pointing to a mark beyond my reach, saying, "When I'm *that* big, I'll be all grown up."

Usually by the time we are eighteen, we are considered "grown up," at least physically. But what about spiritually? Is there an age or a mark we can point to that says, "I'm a spiritual grown-up?" How does spiritual growth take place?

Spiritual growth closely parallels physical growth. We begin as babies when we are "born again" and take in "milk," or the basic teachings of God (Heb. 5:12). After a time, we "leave the elementary teachings about Christ and go on to maturity" (Heb. 6:1).

If we continue to grow in the Lord, we will one day reach a mark called "spiritual maturity." (Spiritual maturity should never be confused with spiritual perfection, which is impossible to achieve in this lifetime.) Part of spiritual maturity is recognizing that no matter how mature we become, there is always room to grow.

Paul says, I press on "to take hold of that for which Christ Jesus took hold of me. Brothers, I do not consider myself yet to have taken hold of it. But one thing I do: Forgetting what is behind and straining toward what is ahead, I press on toward the goal to win the prize for which God has called me heavenward in Jesus Christ." He adds, "All of us who are mature should take such a view of things" (Phil. 3:12-15).

Where are you spiritually? A dependent baby? a self-absorbed teen? a maturing young lady? a wise woman?

You need to know where you are so you can press on in the direction you want to go. You may think, "How can I press on? I can't even stand up! I'm exhausted. Where am I going to find the time and energy it takes to grow spiritually?"

When I say *press on*, I'm not talking about memorizing entire books of the Bible or supervising your church's women's ministry. I'm simply suggesting you go forward in a way that makes sense in your present circumstances.

Press on! Start your day with a prayer. *Press on!* Talk to Jesus about a problem. *Press on!* Memorize one verse. *Press on!* Refuse to wiggle back into habits you've outgrown. *Press on!* Forgive a friend. *Press on!* Persevere through a trial. *Press on!* Set a goal for your future.

It's funny. Amanda, at age six, and I, at, well, let's just say much older, are both pondering what we want to be when we grow up. One day my friend Eileen and I watched as Amanda listened for her dolly's heartbeat with a toy stethoscope. Eileen asked, "Amanda, do you want to be a doctor when you grow up?"

"No," she said. "I want to be a mom."

That's a great goal, Amanda. But can I suggest an

even better goal? The same goal I have for myself . . . to be a mom who loves Jesus.

"Consider it pure joy, my brothers,
whenever you face trials of many kinds,
because you know that the testing of your faith
develops perseverance. Perseverance must finish its
works so that you may be mature and complete,
not lacking anything."
James 1:2-4

Time Out

• Picture yourself when you are eighty years old. What are you like? What qualities do you hope to see in yourself? What can you do now to help yourself be the kind of woman you want to be when you are eighty?

• Set one *realistic* spiritual goal. Share it with a friend. Ask her to hold you accountable in meeting this goal.

• When you face difficulties, do you press on or give up? Use a Bible concordance to locate verses that mention perseverance. Name two Bible characters that demonstrated perseverance. Ask God to develop perseverance in your life.

Copycat

"She's got her mother's nose."

"And eyes."

"And she definitely has Mama's smile . . ."

I couldn't help overhearing comments by neighbors as they cooed over Amanda in the next room. I was flattered to think that my child might share a few of my features. But I knew the truth. Amanda didn't look a thing like me. She *did* have two endearing dimples—but hers were on her face; mine were on my thighs.

As Amanda grew, it was obvious she favored her father in appearance, but she often resembled me in the way she behaved. She was sensitive toward others and enjoyed learning about God . . . and she had an annoying habit of whining when she didn't get her way.

"Mom, Megan is copying me again," Amanda's shrill voice whined from the living room.

Megan mimicked in a quieter, shriller voice, "Mom, Megan is copying me again."

"Stop it!" Amanda ordered, stomping her foot.

"Stop it!" Megan stomped both feet for effect.

"Mommmmm . . ." Amanda marched angrily into the kitchen where I was chopping onions. Megan trotted behind.

"Girls, I'm tired of you teasing each other," I sighed (it sounded like a whine). "Why can't you play together nicely?"

"But Megan copies everything I do and it 'noys me," Amanda pouted.

Megan grinned mischievously. "But, Amanda, I *like* copying you!"

We are all copycats. Little sisters copy big sisters. Big sisters copy parents. Whom do parents copy?

Some copy the Joneses. Others copy sports heroes or television personalities.

Unlike Amanda, the world welcomes us to copy all we want. Movie stars beg, "Use *my* perfume." Educators urge, "Follow these parenting guidelines." Supervisors command, "Do it this way."

But Jesus asks us to copy Him, not the world. "Follow me," Jesus challenges (Matt. 4:19). "I have set you an example that you should do as I have done for you" (John 13:15).

Copying Jesus changes you. Just ask the men and women in Henry Maxwell's congregation who agreed for one year not to make any decision without first asking, "What would Jesus do?"[1] After answering the question, they pledged to respond as they believed Jesus would, regardless of the consequences.

What happened? One man lost his job because he provided court testimony about his company's fraudulent activities. A talented young singer turned down a promising career with an opera company in favor of singing at tent meetings near seedy saloons. A wealthy family canceled their club memberships and funded inner-city projects to help the homeless.

Following Jesus changes your priorities. Wealth, position, power, and appearance lose importance and yield to what really matters—loving God and serving His people.

Question: Why is it so important to copy Jesus?

Answer: Because Jesus copied God.

"I tell you the truth, the Son can do nothing by himself; he can do only what he sees his Father doing, because whatever the Father does the Son also does" (John 5:19).

Jesus was a copycat, but He did more than copy God. He *was* God.

At our home, we often use *Jesus* and *God* interchangeably. When Megan got confused by this, Amanda explained, "Jesus and God are all mixed up together."

That's one way to say it! Jesus said it this way: "I and the Father are one" (John 10:30).

The notion that the One who laid the foundations of the universe would voluntarily confine Himself to a human body is a concept that has confounded great minds. Yet it is so simple a child can understand it.

I explain it to my children this way: "God is your Father. He is good and loving. God wants His children to be like Him. A long time ago, God had some children who were *not* like Him. They were mean and selfish. 'Be good,' God kept telling them, but they didn't listen.

"One day God said, 'Maybe My children would mind Me if they felt closer to Me. I will go to earth and tell them I love them. I will walk among them and show them how I want them to behave.'

"So God became a man called Jesus. Now God's children could touch Him, crawl on His lap, and ask Him questions. Some of His children said, 'I love God. I want to be just like Him.' This made God happy."

Because I love my Father, I too want to be good. Each day I hold up the mirror of Scripture and look into it. Sometimes I see my reflection and think excitedly, *Oh, that's just like my Father!* Other times I see an ugly blemish. *God, remove this and make me more like You,* I pray.

When I first became a Christian, I did not resemble my Father. That's changing. Sometimes I hear someone say the equivalent of, "She's got her Father's heart." Nothing could please me more.

"Be imitators of God . . ."
Ephesians 5:1

Time Out

• It is impossible to copy others if you fail to observe what they say and do. Second Peter 3:18 says, "Grow in the grace and knowledge of our Lord." How can you know Jesus better?

• In I Corinthians 11:1, Paul says, "Follow my example, as I follow the example of Christ." Paul set himself up as a model for others to follow (II Thess. 3:9). Can you think of a mature, godly woman you admire? Ask if she'd be willing to be a "Paul" in your life. Establish a minimum of four meetings together. Take notes on her life and ask her to pray for your spiritual growth.

• For the next week, adopt Henry Maxwell's challenge to his church. Do nothing without first asking, "What would Jesus do?" Then respond accordingly. Share what you learn with a friend.

• What kind of example are you setting for your children? Would you be pleased if they grow up to be just like you?

[1]Charles Sheldon, *In His Steps* (Waco, Texas: Word Books, 1988). This enduring classic will keep your interest even if you can give it only a few minutes at a time.

What Shall We Do with Jesus?

*T*he tree stood tall and proud, forty years of Christmas memories adorning its branches. Twinkle lights blinked cheerfully, illumining silver icicles. Sweet pine perfumed the air.

I stepped back to admire our work. Year after year, the thrill of trimming the tree returned with a freshness that made my heart tingle. I was a little girl again, reliving the wonder of the season through the eyes of my children.

In the background, an angelic choir rang, "Joy to the world, the Lord is come." I hummed with the stereo, praising God for giving the greatest gift the world has ever known.

"Mom, I've been waiting *all* day. Can we do it *now?*" Amanda pleaded.

"Yes, honey. We can do it now." I said.

"Yahooo!" Amanda jumped in the air with cheerleader enthusiasm. She tugged at her baby sister, who was chewing on a red candle. "Come on, Meg! It's time to set up the manger."

I pulled the rickety barn from the box and placed it on the table. Amanda unrolled a body from a cotton mummy casing.

"Be careful, honey," I cautioned. "Remember last year one of the angels got a broken wing."

Three of us sat around the table, stage managers reenacting the greatest moment in history. *Oohs* and *ahhhs* accompanied the unveiling of each character. Even the lowliest had a special role in the wondrous drama.

"You go here." Amanda positioned the shepherd boy on one side of the stable. "And you go there." The wise man, gift in hand, faced the shepherd on the opposite side.

Since this was Megan's first time to "help," veteran manger-setter-upper Amanda appointed herself director. "Mary and Joseph go in the middle of the stable." "The angel belongs on the roof." "NO, Megan! The camel goes *outside.*" "Mom, you're sitting on a cow." (I've been accused of having a cow, but never of *sitting* on one.)

Finally, all the characters were in place. All but one. Megan and I hovered over Amanda as she carefully unwrapped the baby. She looked at the crowded stable. *Oops!* No room in the inn. She looked at me.

"What shall we do with Jesus?" she asked.

Simple question. Complicated answer.

Since the death of Christ 2,000 years ago, the world has been in turmoil over what to do with Jesus. The question has divided nations, toppled governments, ripped apart families. Like an earthquake, the question split the church into hundreds of pieces. Dazed worshipers wandered aimlessly among the rubble, reeling from the aftershocks that came each time the question was asked. Despite attempts at reconstruction, the building process is on hold because workers still cannot agree on what to do with Jesus.

If the question shakes up people today, the tremors were even more pronounced in Jesus' time.

What shall we do with Jesus?

Angels adored Him. Kings bowed before Him. An elderly prophetess worshiped Him.

Nature revered Him. Demons feared Him. Children

cheered Him. Pious pagans steered clear of Him. A prostitute drew near to Him.

Sadducees questioned Him. Herodians harassed Him. Pharisees hated Him.

The house of Jairus laughed at Him. His own family thought Him insane. Peter's family thought Him divine.

Satan tested His humanity. The Holy Spirit proclaimed His deity.

John baptized Him with water. Mary wet His feet with tears. Pilate washed his hands of Him.

A widow gave Him encouragement. A boy offered Him lunch. The government gave Him a bill. The chief priest gave Him guff.

One friend denied Him. Another friend betrayed Him. Enemies whipped Him, spit on Him, stripped Him.

Caiaphas tried Him. Herod defied Him. Romans crucified Him.

A nation despised Him. God glorified Him.

What will *you* do with Jesus? You have three choices. Like the thief who hung on Jesus' left, you can reject Him. Like the thief who hung on His right, you can accept Him. Or, like the Roman leader Felix, you can refuse to make up your mind about Him. Bring Him out front when you want to look respectably religious. Stick Him behind a bale of stable hay when you don't feel like dealing with Him.

I know a few Felixes—people who won't commit. They say, "I'll think about Jesus later," never intending to think about Him at all. The Felixes of the world had better make up their minds, because one day they will have to give an account of what they did with God's Son. Their answer will mean the difference between heaven and hell.

One day every knee shall bow and every tongue confess that Jesus Christ is Lord.

Every knee. Your knee. My knee. Even Felix's knee.

I don't intend to wait for some future day to bow my knee. I'm going to do it today. Right now.

Jesus! I give You center stage in the stable of my heart! I confess Your name. I ask You to be Lord of my life.

That, my friend, is what I will do with Jesus.

What will *you* do with Jesus?

> *"Therefore God exalted him to the highest place*
> *and gave him the name that is above every name,*
> *that at the name of Jesus every knee should bow,*
> *in heaven and on earth and under the earth,*
> *and every tongue confess that Jesus Christ is Lord."*
> *Philippians 2:9-11*

Time Out

• Assume the role of one of the characters at the nativity. Which character did you choose and why? Describe what you see, hear, smell, and feel. What makes this birth different from other births?

• What does it mean to make Jesus Lord of your life? Do you acknowledge Jesus in *every* area of your life? Or do some rooms have a "do not disturb" sign? Are you willing to remove the sign and open the door to Jesus?

• The birth of Jesus is a "joy to the world" year-round. Regardless of the season, pull out your nativity scene and tell your children the story of Jesus' birth.

A Closing Prayer

Dear God,

Sometimes You seem so far off, but after reading this book I realize You are as near as my thoughts. I want to be close to You. I want to think about You, to spend time with You, but I am easily distracted. The baby screams for food. My husband needs me to run to the bank. A friend asks me to watch her son while she goes to the dentist.

So many needs! So much to do! I feel like a lazy Susan spinning round and round with everyone taking something off my shelf. At night, I fall into bed empty and exhausted. Then I groan. In the busyness of the day, I neglected to go to the one person eager to put something *back* on my shelf. You. Forgive me.

Can we start fresh? Beginning now, I will do my best to find—no, to *make*—time to pray and to read Your Word. I know this won't be easy, but I'm determined to make my relationship with You a priority.

Even as I say this, I am aware that I am fragile and prone to lose my focus. Please help me! I can't do this on my own. I need You.

Thank You, Father, for listening, for caring. My heart and my life are Yours.

"Then you will call upon me and come and pray to me, and I will listen to you. You will seek me and find me when you seek me with all your heart." Jeremiah 29:12, 13

How to Have a Personal Relationship with Jesus

If you want the kind of intimate relationship with Jesus discussed throughout this book, but don't know where to begin, here are some suggestions.

AN INTRODUCTION

The first step in knowing Jesus is simply to be introduced to Him. Go to a quiet place by yourself and pray:

• "God, I know I fall short of what You want me to be and that my wrong thinking separates You and me." (See Romans 3:23 and Romans 6:23.)

• "I believe You sent Jesus to pay the price for my sin and that, because He covered my sin, I can have a relationship with You." (See Romans 5:8.)

• "Jesus, thank you for being my Savior. I'd also like you to be my friend." (See John 3:16 and John 1:12.)

BUILDING THE RELATIONSHIP

Now that you and Jesus have been introduced and you've expressed your desire to know Him better, build your relationship with Him just as you would with any friend.

• Spend time together.

• Find out about your Friend. Where did He come from? What does He think? What makes Him happy? sad? Jesus tells you all this in the Bible (the Book of John is a good place to start).

• Talk to Him about your concerns, your hopes, and your dreams.

• Call Him up. You always have a direct line to Jesus through prayer. And He is never too busy to talk with you!

An intimate relationship with Jesus can be the most satisfying relationship you will ever have. Won't you begin today to get to know Him?

Who I Am in Christ

I Am Accepted in Christ

I am God's child.

> Yet to all who received him, to those who believed in his name, he gave the right to become children of God. *John 1:12*

I am Christ's friend.

> I no longer call you servants, because a servant does not know his master's business. Instead, I have called you friends, for everything that I learned from my Father I have made known to you. *John 15:15*

I have been justified.

> Therefore, since we have been justified through faith, we have peace with God through our Lord Jesus Christ, through whom we have gained access by faith into this grace in which we now stand. And we rejoice in the hope of the glory of God. *Roman 5:1*

I am united with the Lord and one with Him in spirit.

> But he who unites himself with the Lord is one with him in spirit. *I Corinthians 6:17*

I have been bought with a price; I belong to God.

> You were bought at a price. Therefore honor God with your body. *I Corinthians 6:20*

I am a member of Christ's body.

> Now you are the body of Christ, and each one of you is a part of it. *I Corinthians 12:27*

I am a saint.

> Paul, an apostle of Christ Jesus by the will of God, To the saints in Ephesus, the faithful in Christ Jesus: *Ephesians 1:1*

I have been adopted as God's child.

> He predestined us to be adopted as his sons through Jesus Christ, in accordance with his pleasure and will. *Ephesians 1:5*

I have direct access to God through the Holy Spirit.

> For through him we both have access to the Father by one Spirit. *Ephesians 2:18*

I have been redeemed and forgiven of all my sins.

> In [Jesus] we have redemption, the forgiveness of sins. *Colossians 1:14*

I am complete in Christ.

> And you have been given fullness in Christ, who is the head over every power and authority. *Colossians 2:10*

I Am Secure in Christ

I am free forever from condemnation.

> Therefore, there is now no condemnation for those who are in Christ Jesus, because through Christ Jesus the law of the Spirit of life set me free from the law of sin and death. *Romans 8:1,2*

I am assured that all things work together for good.

> And we know that in all things God works for the good of those who love him, who have been called according to his purpose. *Romans 8:28*

I am free from any condemning charges against me.

> Who will bring any charge against those whom God has chosen? It is God who justifies. Who is he that condemns? Christ Jesus, who died—more than that, who was raised to life—is at the right hand of God and is also interceding for us. *Romans 8:33,34*

I cannot be separated from the love of God.

> Who shall separate us from the love of Christ? Shall trouble or hardship or persecution or famine or nakedness or danger or sword? *Romans 8:35*

I have been established, anointed and sealed by God.

> Now it is God who makes both us and you stand firm in Christ. He anointed us, set his seal of ownership on us, and put his Spirit in our hearts as a deposit, guaranteeing what is to come. *II Corinthians 1:21*

I am confident that the good work God has begun in me will be perfected.

> . . . being confident of this, that he who began a good work in you will carry it on to completion until the day of Christ Jesus. *Philippians 1:6*

I am a citizen of heaven.

> But our citizenship is in heaven. And we eagerly await a Savior from there, the Lord Jesus Christ. *Philippians 3:20*

I am hidden with Christ in God.

> For you died, and your life is now hidden with Christ in God. *Colossians 3:3*

I have not been given a spirit of fear, but of power, love and a sound mind.

> For God did not give us a spirit of timidity, but a spirit of power, of love and of self-discipline. *II Timothy 1:7*

I can find grace and mercy in time of need.

> Let us then approach the throne of grace with confidence, so that we may receive mercy and find grace to help us in our time of need. *Hebrews 4:16*

I am born of God and the evil one cannot touch me.

> We know that anyone born of God does not continue to sin; the one who was born of God keeps him safe, and the evil one cannot harm him. *I John 5:18*

I Am Significant in Christ

I am the salt and light of the earth.

> You are the salt of the earth. But if the salt loses its saltiness, how can it be made salty again? It is no longer good for anything, except to be thrown out and trampled by men. You are the light of the world. A city on a hill cannot be hidden. *Matthew 5:13,14*

I am a branch of the true vine, a channel of His life.

> I am the true vine, and my Father is the gardener. . . . I am the vine; you are the branches. If a man remains in me and I in him, he will bear much fruit; apart from me you can do nothing. *John 15:1,5*

I have been chosen and appointed to bear fruit.

> You did not choose me, but I chose you and appointed you to go and bear fruit—fruit that will last. Then the Father will give you whatever you ask in my name. *John 15:16*

I am a personal witness of Christ.

> But you will receive power when the Holy Spirit comes on you; and you will be my witnesses in Jerusalem, and in all Judea and Samaria, and to the ends of the earth. *Acts 1:8*

I am God's temple.

> Don't you know that you yourselves are God's temple and that God's Spirit lives in you? *I Corinthians 3:16*

I am a minister of reconciliation.

> Therefore, if anyone is in Christ, he is a new creation; the old has gone, the new has come! All this is from God, who reconciled us to himself through Christ and gave us the ministry of reconciliation: that God was reconciling the world to himself in Christ, not counting men's sins against them. And he has committed to us the message of reconciliation. We are therefore Christ's ambassadors, as though God were making his appeal through us. We implore you on Christ's behalf: Be reconciled to God. *II Corinthians 5:17-20*

I am God's coworker.

> As God's fellow workers we urge you not to receive God's grace in vain. *II Corinthians 6:1*

I am seated with Christ in the heavenly realm.

> And God raised us up with Christ and seated us with him in the heavenly realms in Christ Jesus. *Ephesians 2:6*

I am God's workmanship.

> For we are God's workmanship, created in Christ Jesus to do good works, which God prepared in advance for us to do. *Ephesians 2:10*

I may approach God with freedom and confidence.

> In him and through faith in him we may approach God with freedom and confidence. *Ephesians 3:12*

I can do all things through Christ who strengthens me.

> I can do everything through him who gives me strength. *Philippians 4:13*

Notes

Do you need a speaker for your couples', men's, or women's retreat?

Contact: Pete and Lorraine Pintus,
Hearts at Home Ministries,
4105 Plateau Drive, Colorado Springs, CO 80921
(719) 481-8786.

Are you interested in starting a MOPS group?

Contact: MOPS International
P.O. Box 102200
Denver, CO 80210
(303) 733-5353
(800) 929-1287

Mom

Are you looking for Christian help with parenting?

Chariot Family Publishing has hundreds of books that can help you and your children learn more about the Bible and applying it to your lives.

Look for these educational, inspirational books at your local Christian bookstore.

Close To Home
Fifty-two Devotions to Build Character
in Your Children
by Bonnie Bruno
ISBN 0-7814-0925-X

Mothering
A Christian Approach for Mothers of
All Ages
by Dr. Grace Ketterman
ISBN 0-7814-0150-X

Christian Parenting Answers
Before Birth to Five Years
A Collection from the pages of
Christian Parenting Today magazine
ISBN 0-7814-0182-8